The Kids Drank Pickle Juice

Books by Martie Byrd

Little Ideas, Big Results

The Kids Drank Pickle Juice

The Kids Drank Pickle Juice

Martie Byrd

Shine Like Stars

Copyright 2009 – Martie Byrd

All rights reserved. Printed in the United States of America. No part of this book may be used or reproduced in any manner without written permission except in the case of brief quotations embodied in critical articles and reviews. For information address Shine Like Stars Publishers, 6136 Buckland Mill Road, Roanoke, VA 24019. This book is protected by the copyright laws of the United States of America. Unless otherwise identified, Scripture quotations are taken from the Holy Bible, the New International Version.

ISBN: 978-0-578-02977-1

Dedication

For Carey Smith Even

*Thanks for always being
there to hold my hand.*

Acknowledgements

If weren't for Dave and the kids, I wouldn't have anything to say. I thank and love and bless you. I am indebted to Amy Barringer who sparked the whole idea and who figures prominently!

This book has been improved by the sensitive reading of talented friends to whom I am forever grateful.

Angela Drozdowski, the most thoughtful reader of all.

Don Shires, at the risk of our friendship.

Howard Mermel, universally acclaimed.

Carey Even, who loves everything I do.

Debi Mahler Baum, even though May is as busy as December!

Alexander Maxfield Byrd, Daniel Coope Byrd, Caroline Smith Byrd, livin' the dream.

Thank you to Nicole Lenderking for the cover photograph of her darling Jack, my favorite pickle-lovin' two-year-old.

Much love to my dearest ones: the Smith family, the Byrd family, Friday Night Small Group, the Great Books Club, the Twilight Moms Book Club (for lack of a better name!), the Wooleys, the ATC Bible Study, the Gathering, everyone at Bella magazine and my very sweet Claire Natt. I appreciate you more than words can say.

For the Lord, the lover of my soul. You know....

Roanoke, VA
June 2009

Contents

The Kids Drank Pickle Juice...11

The Lunatics Have Taken Over the Asylum...13

Happy Father's Day to the Cool Parent...16

Buy One, Get One Free...19

The Princess is a Work in Progress...22

My Head Exploded at Wal-Mart Today...25

Feeding Time at the Zoo...30

No Time for a Prodigy...33

I'm Mad at Jamie Lee Curtis...36

Natural Born Leader...38

Mommy's on the Warpath...40

Is Mom the Tooth Fairy?...43

Laptop for Dummies...46

In Defense of Bad Language...49

'Tis the Season (Bah Humbug)...51

Puppy Love...54

Torture at a Middle School Dance...57

Takin' Our Show on the Road...60

Personal Style...63

Wii are Family...66

Makin' the Grade...69

It's All Poop...71

I Found a Miracle in the Dryer...74

Teens, the New Toddlers...76

GPS Kids...79

Shopping Spree...82

Dear Santa...85

Last One on the Bus...88

Honor Your Mother...or Else...90

Wake Up and Smell the Coffee...93

We've Got Short Shorts...96

Freaky Twilight Moms...98

Because I Said So...101

Should I Get Bangs?...104

No Excuses...106

Darn you, Yahoo News!...109

Memory? What Memory?...111

Asked and Answered...115

YahYah in the Jungle...117

You Call That a Compliment?...119

Jesus Took My Acrylic Nails...121

The Mother I Imagined I'd Be...124

I Quit...127

Confessions of a Former Know-It-All...130

How to Make My Lord Your Lord...132

It's Not About Me...135

Who Am I in Christ?...137

My Family

Trevor, Julia, Alex, Caroline and Daniel

Photo by Dave "Happy Daddy" Byrd
Mother's Day 2009

*Meanwhile,
in a little town called Roanoke....*

The Kids Drank Pickle Juice

My friend Amy confided to me one morning. "I'm drowning down here. There are no groceries in the house."

"I am so far behind on laundry that there's no clean underwear. I am wearing my bathing suit bottoms and the kids are going commando."

"The kids who could open jars, did. The kids drank pickle juice! Stop laughing, this is my life! I found Justin drinking pickle juice and Katherine eating peanut butter out of the jar. The babies were gnawing on frozen fish sticks. Thank God it's Monday...only five more days until the weekend," she groaned.

"Dear, dear friend," I intoned. "It won't always be this way. Soon the kids will be able to reach the counter and can make their own sandwiches. They won't drink pickle juice forever. You're in the eye of the storm right now."

"I thought that meant perfect calm?" she interrupted.

"Yes, well, that's when they're all asleep." I reminded.

When moms get together, we inevitably joke about the mothers we imagined we would be versus the mothers we actually are. It's kind of like a Cage Fight: Imaginary Mother vs. Real Mom. The Imaginary Mother is very wimpy and ethereal. She can't hold her own against the mom who has tandem-nursed twins while chasing a toddler into traffic.

Imaginary Mother takes time to shave her legs, keeps up with her hair highlights and whispers, rather than yells, because she read in a parenting bible that it works.

Real Mom dry shaves on the way to the pool, washes her hair before date night and yells because, honestly, sometimes it feels good. She reads the latest theories but doesn't consider them practical. She considered the Bible her parenting guide until the kids baptized it by dropping it in the bathtub. It was super helpful before the pages all stuck together.

Imaginary Mother has no guilt…she's doing everything right. Real Mom struggles with guilt, feelings of inadequacy, fear of the future, envy of other parents and extreme fatigue. And that's all before she gets out of bed in the morning. Real Mom, this book is for you.

Imaginary Mother actually likes field trips and Field Day and room mothering. But here's the secret; she's Imaginary. I'd like Real Mom to know that it is okay to look around your life some days (okay, every day) and say, "Don't we have people for this?" If you've been waiting for people to rescue you from the laundry, the dishes and kids who wipe boogers on the furniture, you're not alone. But you're in for a shock. You are the People you've been waiting for.

One day, you'll look back and laugh. You'll have no choice. This mess is your life and laughter is good medicine. Besides, you've probably cried a few times and noticed that it doesn't change anything. It just scares the kids.

If you've wet your pants when you yelled, or sneezed, or laughed, then this is the book for you. If you are already fairly disgusted because the word "booger" appears on this page, you may as well put the book down. (Later on I say "crap" and I'm not sorry.)

If you need a laugh, love your kids and want to feel less alone, come along for the ride. Having five kids in six years did not qualify me for a reality TV show, only a whole lot of reality. It's real, the stories are real, and they're for you. I hope they make you laugh -- but not so hard you wet your pants. Enough of that already.

The Lunatics Have Taken Over the Asylum

I live at Hormone Central. I'm a forty-ish mom and hormones are messing me up. You know what I'm talking about. Acne and unwanted hair and insane mood swings and chocolate cravings and tears. And that's just on Mondays. But it's not just my hormones. Add to the mix our three teenage sons.

Testosterone drips from the walls in our house. That's some powerful stuff, testosterone. Sure it's cool that they can leap tall buildings in a single bound. Alex, my oldest, does chin ups from the door jams and admires his muscles when he thinks we're not watching. He's almost eighteen…enough said.

Next in line are identical twins who are sixteen. Daniel and Trevor know everything and come in stereo. Think that's enough hormones for one house? Nah! Next, two lovely girls. We have a pre-teen who is almost thirteen and a tweenaged girl aged eleven. Who designates these stages, I don't know. But when Caroline puts her hands on her newly formed hips and assures me that she is a pre-teen, I know not to argue. My baby Julia acts like Hannah Montana and has more earrings than I do. Welcome to my world.

How did I get into this mess? By having five kids in six years. And yes, we did it on purpose. (Sort of.) We wanted a large family and by golly, that's what we got. We had our first three boys in nineteen months. During these early years, I was nearly bald. I imagined that I looked like Demi Moore in *Ghost*. ("Demi Moore in *GI Jane* is more like it," Dave joked.) With three babies, I didn't have time for a shower, never mind a hairstyle. My husband said, "It takes a strong man to be married to a woman with no hair." Who asked him, anyway?

Dave asked on our first date how many kids I wanted to have. Not if I wanted kids…how many. I didn't realize that he was looking for a breeder. Clearly he wanted to carry on the Byrd traits. Boy, did he. Child after child came out as mini-Daves. They all arrived with the same checklist. Blonde hair? Check. Pointy chin? Check. Porcelain skin? Check. My mother took a look at each baby and uttered, "Ah, another Byrd." I was the human incubator, turned laundress, chief cook and house elf. Ah, the joys of motherhood.

Back when Dave probed about how many of his children I'd like to have, I answered, "As many as we could emotionally and financially handle." Now we laugh and say, "And then we had four more." See, now that we have a houseful of teens, we realize that we can't handle it. But it's too late. You can't put them back. They're too big. Plus, my abdominal muscles are shot and most of them could easily carry me around for nine months, instead of the reverse.

I have finally reached the age when I realize I don't know it all, but guess what? Now my kids do. They know everything and I don't. Stupid, stupid, stupid Mom. My sweet teen Trevor constantly argues. When he was fourteen, he argued with me about the day of his birth. He remembers it better than I do. He actually said that. He believes it, too. Do you see what I am dealing with?

I write to set the record straight. Read on and then you, sympathetic reader, can take my side. Someone has to take my side. You see, when I think of life at home with all these kids/hormones/opinions, one phrase comes to mind: The Lunatics Have Taken Over the Asylum.

Thanks to my hormones, I'm at that age when I can't remember a single thing. But here's the problem. The lunatics, er, kids in my house, have figured that out. They use my absent-mindedness against me. They know it all…and remember everything. My eldest just told me this week, "You stink at math and you have a bad memory." Ah, what a sweet line.

Remember when they used to think that Mommy hung the moon and stars? He's the first one to get out of trouble by asserting, "But I told you where I was going!"

Did he tell me? I can't remember. Their hormones give them courage. My hormones give me confusion. See how it's toxic? And a whole lot of fun. Turnabout is fair play, or so they say. My kids are already writhing in humiliation that I am writing about them. Ha hah ha ha! This might be the best thing I've ever done in my life.

I love being a mom. I really do. It's a joy, challenge and adventure. Why climb Everest when you can be a mother? Same thrills, risks and rewards. Motherhood causes me to burst with pride, grin like the Cheshire cat and pluck myself bald on a daily basis. I never want it to end and I never want to forget a thing. Watch my little bundles as they grow up and leave the nest. So come along for the adventure. I'd really appreciate the company.

Happy Father's Day to the Cool Parent

I met my husband, Dave, on a plane. I was sitting in his seat but instead of telling me to beat it, he said, "Are you sitting there?" That suave pick-up-line has lived in infamy. Over time he said, "You're in my seat, you know." I told him that was impossible since I don't make mistakes. Famous last words. Comparing our boarding passes showed that he was actually correct. I had indeed made a mistake…my first. I still maintain that the seat numbers were askew and there was nothing I could have done. (Blurred vision due to a free margarita bar the night before perhaps contributed to this first error.)

A week later, Dave drove from his home in Annapolis, Maryland to my shabby rental in Philadelphia, Pennsylvania to take me out to lunch. From this I concluded that he was very hungry for a cheesesteak or he actually liked me. Later that same day he asked me The Question: "How many children would you like to have?"

Note, that he did not ask if I wanted kids but "How many?" A staunch feminist, I still went out with him again. What the heck, he was cute…and he drove 120 miles to see me. We met at Thanksgiving, got engaged that St. Patrick's Day and were married just after Labor Day. His biological clock was ticking and we didn't have any time to waste. We had a big family to make!

Dave was one of those guys who always knew he wanted to have kids. It simply took him a few years to find the perfect woman to have them with. He waited thirty-six years to meet me. (The year he enlisted in the Air Force, I enlisted in 4th grade.) Due to advanced paternal age, we started our family as soon as was decent.

A natural father, Dave has always been a master of rough-housing, funny voices and "Sure, you can stay up later." Not a big one for rules, he's a pro at having fun. We had our three sons in our first two years of marriage. Big brother Alex was joined by twins Danny and Trevor and that got the party started. By then Dave and I really knew each other…for better or for worse.

I was a severely Type A mom who alphabetized my spices, kept a freezer inventory, and labeled all the toy bins. Race cars, Duplos and plastic dinosaurs each had their own bin. My kids could not open a toy bin without my permission. I refused to allow co-mingling of toys. Back then, I didn't realize that Dave was one of the boys…and that he was perfectly capable of opening the toy bins.

The first time I left him alone with the three boys, I came home to a huge mountain of toys. Dave had opened all the bins! And dumped them out in the middle of the room! When I started crying, he said, "We'll pick them up." He went into the garage, got a snow shovel and proceeded to scoop the co-mingled toys back into the bins.

I wondered if perhaps we should have dated a wee bit longer before starting a family together. I am a planner. Dave is spontaneous. I am an organizer. Dave is relaxed. I am a driver. Dave is a napper. I thank God for Dave. If it weren't for Dave, our kids wouldn't have had any fun at all!

Now that we have a houseful of teens, they thank God for their dad, too. If it were up to me, I'd still be choosing their clothes, brushing their teeth and reading them bedtime stories. Dad is the one who takes them white water rafting and skiing on Black Diamond slopes. Dad lets them stay up until all hours watching TV. He snuck the first game system into the house and got them cell phones when each turned twelve. In short, he's the cool one.

But he's not just fun and games. No, Dad teaches them to finish what they've started. He has shown devotion to our family and to God. Most of all, Dad helps them with math homework. Where would we be without Dad? Happy Father's Day, you crazy dude. I'm thankful to US Air for bringing us together. I appreciate your humor and the fact that you've helped me to loosen up. I know the kids appreciate it, too. To celebrate your big day, go ahead and take a nice nap. We'll wake you when we need you to start the grill.

Buy One, Get One Free

If I had a dollar for every time someone said to me, *"I always wanted to have twins!"* I might be able to afford mine. Buy One, Get One Free....if only that was true. Double the kids, double the cash; that's the reality. The only exception to this rule was the insurance co-pay for their birth. One mom = one co-pay. We got our pair for the low, low price of $10. I've had sunscreen that cost more.

Twins carry with them a great deal of fascination in our culture and around the world. I call this The Freak Factor. I'm allowed to do that. See, I'm a Freak myself. Surprised? Yes, it's true. I have a twin myself. I'm a twin...and I have twins. We could call that Freak Factor, Squared. Or perhaps we could call it The Freak Factory. There are some important differences, however. My sister Carey and I are fraternal twins. We each had our own uterine apartments aka sacks. Daniel and Trevor are identical twins. That means they've been getting in each other's business since conception.

Identical twins are a random biological occurrence around the world. Only 8% of twins are identical twins. Only God knows why the egg splits; it's a medical mystery! (No, they don't skip a generation or come because your husband's uncle had a twin.) Because they are the result of a fertilized egg that splits, they have a lot in common. They share fingerprints. They share DNA. They share....well, that's about it. Once they're in the world, they don't care to share. At least mine don't.

By the time I was a teenager, I found it difficult to be a twin. Think about it. When you're a teenager, you crave your own unique identity. It's an age when you barely want to acknowledge that you come from a family, never mind from a matched set. Most teens would prefer their peers think they sprung fully formed from a cabbage patch. They fantasize about being raised by wolves.

To them, all the parental love and attention is frankly disgusting. *"No, Mom, you don't need to come to the awards ceremony, geez, leave me alone."* This is especially true of teenage boys who wish they were raised like Tarzan who didn't have a mom to bug him to shower and change his loincloth.

When you have a sibling in your school, it is like the Seventh Layer of Hell for most teens. Put that sibling in all of your classes and you've got the recipe for miserable. Then, to make it really, really bad, make sure you look just like the other kid. Similar enough so that all day, every day, teachers, staff and your best friends say, *"Which one are you?"* Feel like running away from home yet? Yup, it's hard. I sympathize with my guys. I could tell you an annoying twin story or two. Here's one.

My sister and I used to argue on school mornings about our outfits. She would get up at six a.m. to shower and dress. I would hit the snooze alarm until seven a.m. I'd leap up, minutes before it was time to leave the house. I'd throw on my bargain basement Jordache jeans and the first Fair Isle sweater I saw. Sometimes, however, she was already wearing her $55 Calvin Klein's and a Fair Isle. She would not be seen in public looking anything like me. Wars would ensue over who had to go change their clothes. The one who put on the sweater first? Or the one who put it on last?

One memorable morning, our War of the Argyles was unresolved as we entered the hallowed halls of our preppy New England high school. Seeing Carey between classes, I took advantage of the opportunity to give her a swift kick. Unfortunately, the principal bore witness to this ladylike scene. He called me over for a reprimand, which I interrupted with this explanation, *"It's okay, she's my twin."* Oddly, he didn't think it was okay. (Clearly he was a single birth or in the twin vernacular, a singleton.)

That's just a peek into what it's like to be a twin in high school. And remember, we don't even look alike. Now take Danny and Trevor Byrd. They look alike. They have the added challenge of going to a small school. And, did I mention, they are identical?

They look so alike that they are constantly seeking ways to differentiate themselves. They have changed their hair style and color more often than Britney Spears on a bender. I am sympathetic. Having your very own facial features is something most of the world takes for granted. They are singletons at heart, yet stuck with a twin brother. Oh, how they'd like to break free!

When I told the boys I was going to write about them, Danny wanted to make sure I mentioned that they are single. Well, they are double, but available. See what I mean? It's confusing. Think twice before you fill that prescription for Clomid, that's all I'm saying…..

The Princess is a Work in Progress

The other day, I was playing hooky with my daughter Caroline. She was enjoying an infrequent but much-deserved Mental Health Day off from school. She's getting older, so it's slightly more challenging, not to mention more expensive, to find an activity she'd enjoy. It used to be that a container of bubbles or Play-Doh provided hours of magic. Not anymore. Now she's asking to get a Mocha at Starbucks or go for a pedicure. This day we decided to go paint our own pottery. It's fun, you get something cool to use and it's great mother-daughter bonding time.

Since it was noontime on Thursday, there were only a few other women there. Actually, the other occupied table held three generations of women: grandmom, a mom and a birthday girl, just turned two. I could not tear my eyes away from the little one. (I'm sure I made her mom nervous). You see, she was the spitting image of my Caroline ten years prior. The spitting image. I felt like I was in both ends of a Time Machine.

Sweet Caroline was an adorable baby. She had a perfectly round face, gigantic blue eyes, and fluffy white-blonde curls. More than once, people would comment, "She doesn't even look real." I joked that she was our mail order baby and that we had paid extra for "sleeps through the night" and a premium for "doesn't fuss, even when wet, hungry or tired." After having three boys, you can't imagine how much we paid for the girl features! She looked like a living doll and what's better, she acted like one.

This little girl, Sarah, was just that cute. She was well-behaved and simply precious. Can you imagine bringing a two-year old to a pottery store? In a pink fur vest? And letting her paint? To me, inviting a toddler to a room full of breakables and leaving with everything intact is a fantasy. It's the definition of well-behaved.

Her sweet young mom was painting a lovely plaque for Sarah's room. I remember when I used to be that thoughtful. This was before my kids took markers to the walls. Even precious Caroline drew imaginary friends on the walls of her room. Maybe this little Sarah won't get a hold of the Sharpies. Her pretty pink room will stay tidy and on her door in a place of honor will be a sign announcing that the Princess lives here.

On this day, however, Sarah was getting hungry, so Mom wasn't able to finish the princess plaque. She asked if she could come finish it later, saying, "The princess is a work in progress."

Truer words were never spoken. Wise, wise words. She was referring to the painted piece. I was thinking of the child. Truly, the Princess is a Work in Progress. That day, I saw my princess at age two and age twelve and peered at age twenty-two down the road. You see, it's not the pottery project that's a work in progress. It's the whole Princess.

It takes a lot to raise these little people. Time, patience, cash money and lots of Mental Health Days for both moms and kids. How do we get from a two-year-old painting pottery, through the minefield of teen years, to a healthy, vibrant bride? It's a work in progress.

After four children, my fertile friend Amy is contemplating another baby and she said to me, "It's just another nine months."

I kept my mouth shut for about ten seconds, and then I blurted out, "It's not nine months! It's twenty-one years and half a million dollars!" But even that is a quick summary. After all, it's easy to have a baby; it's hard to raise a child. There are no words in our language to communicate parenting. Work in progress is at least a start.

The Princess is a Work in Progress. Bless you, my little Caroline, turning big Caroline, with poise and intellect. I see little Sarah in you, in your glowing cheeks and still clear skin. I see myself in you, when you sit on your bed, writing in a journal like I did thirty years ago. If I squint my eyes, I can see you on your wedding day. I see that you will not only outlive me, you will out succeed me and I rejoice.

You're a young teen, an age when you still admire me. I know from experience that will change. I turned against my parents, and your brothers have often turned against me. I ask, Caroline, that you hold off your hormones until your brothers are further down the time machine. Then, continue on through. It's part of the plan….part of the work in progress.

For now, whenever you leave me, I call after you, "Make good choices." And whisper under my breath…"Princess."

My Head Exploded at Wal-Mart Today

If you need kitty litter, a hairbrush, some pansies for the garden, two gallons of milk and something for dinner, you have no choice. None. You have to go to Wal-Mart. That's just all there is to it. There is no other store where you can reasonably purchase these items.

However, take it from me. It's not going to be pretty. Exhibit A: my recent trip. I allowed myself one hour to pick up this very small list from the Superstore near me. I was determined to have a laser focus and not wile away the hour looking at the discounted bakery items, wondering if it was decadent to buy a slightly stale birthday cake for no good reason. I was going to Get In and Get Out. Armed with a list and meaning business, I approached the store.

And headed straight for the bathroom. There is something about shopping that irritates my bladder, apparently, because I always have to go when I get there. I liked it when my kids were potty training because then it would appear to be their issue, not mine, when we had to beg to use the facilities. Not every store is anxious for you to share in their Employees Only bathroom. But Wal-Mart is designed with two bathrooms: one up front and one in the back of the store.

They have two bathrooms but apparently they are not expecting company because the bathrooms are usually filthy. (I don't want Wal-Mart to sue me or anything; I'm just stating my personal observations from perhaps five hundred trips to their can.) Generally I have to pass several stalls before I find one that I can use without having to update my vaccinations. I do my business as efficiently as possible and scurry to the door. I always wonder if it's perhaps more germy to wash my hands at their sink than not wash my hands at all. But, like all women, I wash my hands because I know other women are watching to see if I'm washing them. I draw the line at the hot air hand dryer. I'm sure it's spewing out Swine Flu. I dry my hands on my pants and get ready to shop.

Savvy Wal-Mart shoppers have already noticed something about my list. The items I need are perfectly positioned at opposite corners of the store. Unfortunately, I am wearing the new shoes that rub me in all the wrong places. This will hamper my fast walking, but I am not deterred. I mentally put the pansies on the bottom of my list. I may not be able to handle the Garden Center today.

Traversing the store, I determine to start in the way back where the milk is located. Why is the milk in the back of the store? This means it is already warm before I've even checked out! Are we supposed to start at the front of the store and do the Milk and Dairy last? If so, why aren't the registers in the back of the store? I know this is an evil plot to get me to spend more time in the store and spend more money. And it works. But, I digress… I blister-walk to the cold section and pick up two gallons of 2% milk. Heck, since I'm here anyway, I should stock up. I add the 1% milk that Danny drinks and the Lactose-free milk that Julia drinks. I pick up two gallons of skim milk for Caroline and me. Look! Wal-Mart has the best price on the hazelnut flavored creamer that Dave likes so much. He shuns the low-fat or sugar-free varieties. He likes what we lovingly refer to as "fatty fat boy creamer." I throw some of those in. What the heck.

Next, something for dinner. I settle on bratwurst. It's a family favorite since our days of living in Chicagoland. Two packages for $6, that's a steal! I pick up four packages. I'll freeze two. Then I remember that Danny doesn't eat bratwurst and I throw in some hot dogs. We're into health food. Walking past that section, I recall also that the kids need some things for lunch and corn dogs are a favorite. I get a case. Yum yum, twenty-four corn dogs. We consider any type of processed meat or meat by-products as health food at our house. I limp up to the bread section to get the rolls to go with the brats. (The meat, not the kids.)

In a nod to good health (and yes, I see the irony here), I like to get the whole wheat buns. My favorite is double fiber whole wheat buns; these make me feel like Mother of the Year for the good I'm doing for my kids' colons. However, the white flour/high fructose corn syrup ones are $1 for twelve buns. The whole wheat will set me back $2.49 for six buns. I buy one bag of whole wheat (for me and my colon) and one bag of white. Eighteen buns...a crazy purchase. This meal is getting expensive. But time is ticking away, I've already spent thirty minutes at Wal-Mart, I've got to keep rolling.

My intention is to pass the produce on my way to pick up the hairbrush, but the strawberries are on sale, so I grab a few packs. Dave has been complaining I'm not buying the apples he likes because I confuse Gala with Fuji. They are both apple names with four letters and I'm easily confounded. I tell him if he'd only like Pink Ladies, I would remember that. This deliberation takes three minutes and ends with a stalemate. I grab a bag of prepackaged apples; if no one eats them, I'll make a pie. Off to the hairbrush aisle.

Buying a new hairbrush is tricky. The best way to see if you like the bristles would be to actually brush your hair with it. Of course, this is also the best way to get lice. Brushes come in a wide variety of color and price points, too. My hairdresser told me I needed a soft bristle vented brush. I don't see that among the hundreds here at Wal-Mart. Next time I'll just buy a $25 brush at the salon when she is there to assist me. The decision is too much for me to make and the pansies are calling my name from a few aisles down. However, I do remember the kids need shampoo in their bathroom so I throw in the Suave that's on sale, remembering to match the shampoo and conditioner. No one likes to wash their hair with Green Apple then condition it with Coconut. I've made that error before!

Fifteen minutes to go. Plenty of time for pansy shopping. This involves pushing my now heavy cart to the outside patio area. My Wal-Mart does not have an automatic door leading to the outdoors. Instead it has a petulant cashier who seems to enjoy watching people with shoes that are much too small try to persuade their processed meat laden cart over a door jamb in an effort to look at flowers in the outdoor Garden Center. She won't lift a hand to help but instead sneers at me as she talks to her boyfriend on her cell phone.

The pansies are cheerful, though, and definitely worth the effort. I grab the whole flat, in the interest of time, and because I've learned that it's insanity to try to mix and match for color, health, bloom ability and the like. All purple is fine. If some are dead, also fine. The flat fits nicely on the under part of the carriage. My right foot is now bleeding from the blister and… that's right! I forgot the kitty litter! I must navigate the trick door back into the store and backtrack to Pet Supplies. Darn, this means my sneering cashier will not get to ring up my Suave, milks, brats and the rest. She would have really enjoyed doing that, too.

As I march along, the tray of pansies slides south and they dump onto the ground. Cell phone Cashier gives me a withering look but does not interrupt her call to help me. Of course not, how silly of me to even consider that. I hobble back to Pet Supplies and buy a gigantic bucket of kitty litter. I can't wait until the warmer weather so our cats can use the sandbox. (Stop groaning! The kids have outgrown the sandbox, what else is it good for? This way I don't have to scoop the litter box.) Time is up! And I still have to check out.

I evaluate all the lines and pick one with only one person in front of me. I have ten minutes to check out in order to still be on time for the kids getting off the bus. Ten minutes seems like more than enough time to check out at Wal-Mart. Unless you are me, that is. It seems that I always chose the line with the employee who is in training. The person ahead of me has several items of clothing that are missing tags and needs a snail to run a price check. Oh yes, he also wants a certain brand of menthol cigarettes which are only available in Lane 36. A sloth will go get those.

My heart rate elevates during this cheery exchange. I am trailing dirt from the pansies and blood from my blisters. That's what I get for buying my shoes from Goodwill. I can feel my blood pressure rising. I now have five minutes. Four. Three. Two. UNLESS I CHECK OUT THIS INSTANT, I WILL NOT BE HOME IN TIME FOR THE BUS. Their items all tallied…just hand 'em the receipt and ARE YOU KIDDING ME? The register tape is out. This will be another interminable delay. My brains explode all over the register, the Wal-Mart bags, and the now warm milk I am buying.

At least, that what it feels like every time I go to Wal-Mart. Ten torturous minutes later, I am sprinting across the parking lot, trying to make up for lost time. I frantically throw the milk, bread, strawberries, pansies, and why-didn't-I-get-any-old-brush-it's-what-I-came-for, in the back of the van. I return the cart to the kiosk and notice that the kitty litter is shoved to the back of the cart. I have to get on my knees to retrieve it. The economy pail crushes my whole wheat rolls and topples over on the pansies. I get home just as the bus is pulling up. The bus driver frowns at me. She looks an awful lot like the lady who works in the Garden Center.

This is why I pray before I step foot in a Wal-Mart. And it also explains why I'm functioning with less gray matter than the rest of you.

Feeding Time at the Zoo

Family Dinners. Researchers tout them as the Magical Childrearing Solution. Simply eat dinner with your family (and without the TV!) at least five nights a week. Here's what you'll get in return. Family Dinners are reported to reduce teenage alcoholism and drug use, increase self-image and vocabulary, and maintain healthy weights. You may think I'm exaggerating but go ahead and Google it yourself. In families who eat dinner together, the children are stronger, smarter and happier. It doesn't matter what you eat, as long as you eat it together.

We have family dinner five or six nights a week. (Sunday is the Sabbath and I simply feel that that "no work on the Sabbath" applies to slaving over the hot stove. Don't you agree?). Dinnertime with our teens and preteens is a stew of conversations about their day, shared values aka lecture), laughter, scolding, schedule coordination and sometimes a few tears (over spilled milk, etc). Very, very infrequently do we invite visitors into our ritual. You'll soon read why.

When I was growing up, my father used dinnertime as an opportunity to school us on our manners. One of six children, I came later in life when my parents were getting tired of the constant repetition of "Please get your elbows off the table." Instead, Dad just poked our elbows with his fork. Perhaps not very sanitary, but it was highly effective. In our home growing up, not a single child would dare to even pick up our fork until our mother, the hostess, began eating. We knew better.

I imagined that my own five beautiful children would absorb manners through osmosis, just by observing their very proper parents. After all, we use our napkins, wait to be served, pass right to left, and use our quiet inside voices. Osmosis? YEAH RIGHT! For many (many, many!) years dinnertime was simply crowd control. We had our kids in a big litter and we were exhausted. We dished out the mac-n-cheese as fast as they could eat it with their chubby, grimy toddler hands. We knew we'd have to teach them manners one day, but we reacted like Scarlett O'Hara in *Gone with the Wind*. "I'll think about that tomorrow" was our mantra...for about twelve years.

I wish we had started earlier. We've got some teens with atrocious manners and I'm afraid no one will marry them. Now is the time to pay the piper. Like my father before me, I think dinnertime is a great time to review the standards of common decency. Therefore, every night at about 6 p.m., the years of my father's mannerly tutelage come rushing back. I start to work on these pigs, er, Byrds, and their table manners.

Recent lesson include:

Introduction to Table Settings.

No, it's not right to dump a pile of forks in the middle of the table and fight over them! And no sword fighting...period!

Napkin Use 101.

Please wipe your hands on your napkin instead of your pants! The laundry lady is begging you!

Date Menu 201.

Watching you eat spaghetti is making me sick and I'm your mother. I'm warning you, don't ever order that on a date.

Although our five children are very smart, they are oddly resistant to this line of instruction. I can see where my wise dad concluded that the fork pretty much said it all.

Don't get me wrong. We have a fun time at the dinner table. There's generally a lot of merriment. But these are teenagers and they haven't been allowed out of the house very much. A wise mother once encouraged me by saying, "Don't worry.

When the boys see how their potential girlfriends react to their table manners, they'll straighten right out." I look forward to that day. But in the meanwhile, it can get pretty darn awkward when we invite company to dinner.

For instance, the other day our daughter Julia invited her friend Jenna to stay for dinner. Mayhem ensued. The chairs were scraped lazily across the floor. Only three place settings included both a fork and a knife. One person had hiccups, one person threw a roll as an expedited way of passing it to the sibling across the table and one of my little lovelies could not contain several very loud belches.

"I'm so sorry, sweetie," I apologized sincerely to Jenna who only has her well-mannered sister Elena at home.

"That's alright, Mrs. Byrd," she replied, "My dog has very bad manners, too."

That about sums it up. The Byrds are akin to the dog that begs for table scraps, runs off with the Thanksgiving turkey, eats the contents of the bathroom wastebasket and is, for pity's sake, an animal. Feeding time at the zoo. Would you care to join us? I don't think Jenna will be back.

No Time for a Prodigy

Recently I took time away from my busy laundry schedule to drive a bunch of sophomores on a field trip.

We went to the ballet. I sat in between two of my favorite lively tenth graders…Mark on my left, Alex on my right. Alex is my oldest son. He's not yet seventeen but he has facial hair like Wolverine and a manly deep voice, too. I imagined this seating arrangement would keep everyone happy and I waved merrily to the other chaperones as the show began. To introduce the production, the Director called out some Tiny Dancers. They were in elementary school but announced that they had been dancing for years and years…and years.

As the lights dimmed, Alex leaned over to me and dropped this bomb. "I could have been something, you know. If only you had encouraged me, I would have been good at something by now." The curtain opened as I squeaked out in dismay, "Did you want to dance?"

In an audible (read: REALLY LOUD AT THE BALLET) voice, he replied, "No, but I was a prodigy at gymnastics. You never encouraged me."

For this I'm skipping my laundry duty? I fumed all the way through the performance. Is this my legacy? I've created scrapbooks of every report card, art project and potty training picture, but I haven't encouraged you? Is that the accusation? I sat through decades of T-ball games, laughed at thousands of knock-knock jokes and told you I loved you every single day of your life. Not encouraging? I was speechless.

After the performance, I shared the story with two mom friends. I guess I was a teensy, weensy bit upset. I'm afraid I was ranting. "Prodigy!" I sputtered. "We didn't have time for a prodigy!" The moms laughed uproariously at my declaration.

One friend, let's call her Mrs. Smith (because that's her name), laughed, "You didn't have TIME for a PRODIGY! HAHAHAH! Good one! You are hilarious!"

Here's the thing. I wasn't kidding.

We had five kids in six-ish years. Alex really <u>was</u> a gifted young athlete. He sat up at three months old, unassisted. At nine months old, he scaled the toy cupboard. I counted to three, meaning, "You're in trouble now, buster." When I got to three, he jumped. He was fearless.

At age two, he could do the hand-over-hand at the playground. Without diapers, he was so skinny his pants fell down around his ankles. He kept going. His dad and I watched crowds form. One kid yelled, "Hey, it's Amazing Boy! That kid is amazing!" We still call him Amazing Boy around the house. With different parents, and fewer siblings, he could be on his way to the Olympics right now. But that was not to be.

I'm sorry, Alex. You are the oldest of five. We simply had no time for a prodigy. Breakfast, lunch and dinner consumed all of our energy for years. Now it's up to you to shine. If you're going to be stellar at something, it's gonna have to start now, when you can drive yourself there. Yes, you heard me. Now that you have a driver's license, feel free to Go for the Gold. Just consider this. If your Pursuit of Prodigy is going to be expensive, you'd better get a second job. Mom's just trying to keep gas in the tank, you know what I mean?

No time for a prodigy. I'm serious. Both Dave and I decided early on that we were okay with Slightly Above Mediocre for our darlings. We don't have a smidgen of Stage Mom or Dad in our DNA. Those dedicated parents who get up at 4 a.m. to drive their child to an audition in Manhattan? No, that wouldn't be us. The ones who sit at the ice rink freezing to death for years on end? Nope, can't hack it. The parents who consider an outing to be a trip to the library and perhaps a soft-serve cone? Now that's more like it.

Now that the teens are getting older, however, I'm ready for evidence of excellence. I tried to explain to dear Alex that he can still be a prodigy. He's in the early chapters of his life story. Be a prodigy all you want! Go ahead, excel at something. And when you succeed, please don't go on Oprah and blame your poor mother who simply did the best she could.

When confronted with this essay, Alex said, "Oh Mom, I was only kidding."

I'd like that in writing, please.

I'm Mad at Jamie Lee Curtis

.....and we've never even met.

You see, a few years back, actress Jamie Lee Curtis allowed herself to be photographed without any make-up. And, gasp, in bicycle shorts. She had the muffin top that so many of us sport. The photo was not retouched or altered in any way. Google it yourself. The article was called *True Thighs*.

If you have to ask, you probably don't have one. A "muffin top" is the fat that spills over a waistband that's too tight. It is aptly named as it is indeed the product of too many of those mega-muffins they sell at Sam's Club. It's a common occupational hazard of moms. I know how I got mine. It was from eating off of five kids' lunch plates while telling myself that I would save calories by not having lunch. I also convinced myself that if I ate while I was moving, I was simultaneously burning calories. That was my favorite excuse. Finally, for years I believed and told other people that if you talked while you ate you would not gain weight. Sigh, if only it was true.

Jamie Lee had a muffin top and a goofy grin in the picture. The reason she did it was to expose the ridiculous airbrushing and retouching done on every celebrity's picture. She wanted us to know that is not reality. She let us see how she really looked. We're all in it together, she was saying, long before *High School Musical* coined the phrase.

She was grinning. I loved that photograph. For about five years it made me feel better about myself. I actually looked like Jamie Lee Curtis. (Only around the midsection but hey, it's a start.) Recently, however, I read an article where Jamie says she's sorry she ever did that photograph. Now she says that people took it the wrong way. She didn't really mean we should all be comfortable with our bodies.

These days, Jamie is a spokesmodel for the yogurt that introduces the good bacteria into our guts. That's her thing now. She's organic. The new article said that she fears she will be better known for the muffin top shot than any other photograph. She has gotten back on the elliptical and lost twenty pounds. Her kids are older now so I suppose she stopped noshing on all those Goldfish and went back to eating sushi. So now I'm mad at Jamie Lee Curtis.

Here's what I want Jamie Lee to know. Jamie, we loved it. You were so real. So true. So authentic. Don't go all South Beach on us, Jamie. We thought you were one of us.

True beauty comes from within, right? Inner beauty is revealed when we take off the mask of perfection that we are desperately trying to hold up. Do you have moments, like Jamie Lee did, when you drop the mask? When you reveal your inner self to a friend, a sister, a daughter? You go, girl.

Let her out! Let her out, Jamie Lee! Let her out, Martie! Let her out, insert-your-name-here! And then, celebrate! I'm celebrating with you right now! Hurray for you! Do it more often. Be real. And don't ever, ever regret being more authentic. Don't turn back, like Jamie Lee, and try to erase the lesson you have shared. That's just uglier than a muffin top, really.

See, each time we reveal an inner weakness, share an embarrassing moment, or discuss a deep fear, we become stronger. We all realize that we are much more alike than we are different. And that's really beautiful.

Natural Born Leader

Recently Trevor had an awesome opportunity. He was able to go to a HOBY Youth Leadership Summit. It came up unexpectedly. The brilliant 4.0 scholar who was slated to go was suddenly expected at a horse show. The slot was open. Trevor saw the opportunity and jumped at it. Who wouldn't? It was an all-expense paid weekend at a college campus with a bunch of other high school sophomores. There was a three to one girl to guy ratio. He was there.

Being my father's daughter, I was there an hour early. The meeting was held at the beautiful University of Richmond campus. My parents had brought me to visit that campus about twenty-five years prior. A Connecticut Yankee, I had an obsession with the South since I read *Gone with the Wind* in fifth grade. I wanted to go to a southern school but in the end, I didn't pick U of R. They had a lake separating the guy's campus from the girl's campus. I was much too boy crazy to agree to that landscaping.

I was in a Time Machine. I could see myself as a high school student visiting the campus. I could see and feel that so clearly. But I could also see my child about to embark on his own college experience. It was a mind warp. The trip reminded me of the sacrifices my parents made. They sent each of their six children to private, four-year colleges. The closer I get to sending my kids to college, the more I appreciate my parents. This was only a three-day weekend, but also a dry-run. Would I have what takes to leave my boy at a university and drive away? The future was right there, right across the ancient stone threshold. My emotions were at an all-time high.

Trevor had an awesome weekend. We didn't know he was slated to be there, but God did. God plucked him away from surfing the 'net and updating his Facebook status in order to show him something. Trevor saw the big world outside our doors. He was blind but now he sees.

Trevor fit in with those chosen leaders. He was picked to star in the skit. He led the break dancing during the dance. For the first time ever, he was not known as one of the Byrd Boys or one of the twins or even as our son. He was there as himself. Trevor starred as Trevor. He didn't want to leave.

The weekend changed him. He even looked different to us when we came to get him. He looked taller. Older. More confident. He wasn't the same kid we dropped off on Friday. He was a leader on Sunday, a young man with a dream, a kid who had found purpose. It was a crazy payoff for what was to us a free weekend.

On the way to the summit, Trevor told me his life plans. He had decided that after high school, he was going to go to community college and continue to work at Chick-fil-A. On the way home, his dream had shifted. He wanted to go to University of Richmond or another college that attracted young leaders. He expected more of himself and his future. He could see himself achieving, volunteering, leading. It shifted my dreams for him, too. In just one weekend, I had to shift from good-enough to go-for-it.

He broke down on the way home. Suddenly he realized he had two more years at home. He likes his family but we can't hold a candle to a dorm and a roommate and all-you-can-drink Dr. Pepper in the cafeteria. He wanted to be there today... but it's a tomorrow place to be.

Hold on, Trevor. Your future is bright. Walk into it step by step. Do your homework and dream your dreams. God knows you are going to be a star.

Mommy's on the Warpath

I just changed my zillionth roll of toilet paper since summer began. No exaggeration. There are seven bums in my family. Yes, I meant bums and not one of them can stoop to conquer the toilet roll replacement. This steams my corn, if you know what I mean.

I am especially bothered by the non-roll replacement when I notice too late. Naturally, no one has refilled the tissue box, either. Can you hear my yelling for some aid? Right, no one in my house hears my desperate cries, either.

This type of non-help is especially aggravating to me during the lazy, hazy days of summer. You would think having five kids out of school would be sort of like having a small legion of household help. You would think. Sadly, I have observed that the opposite is true.

They seem to think I am here to serve them. They eat in the family room within hours of Stanley Steamer leaving us a $300 bill for carpet cleaning. They unabashedly leave evidence of their midnight snacks. They expect me to believe that every night, a bunch of starving sprites invade our home and leave ice cream dishes, chip wrappers and empty soda cans bandied about willy nilly. When I come downstairs in the morning, I am cheerful....for about ninety seconds. Before I can sit down for my daily Bible reading, I am sidetracked by the Mardi Gras-like mess left from the night before. I am usually yelling at someone -- anyone -- before I've had my first cup of coffee for the day.

Welcome to my world. It's a mess. Someone left remnants of Cookies 'n' Cream ice cream in the downstairs lavatory the other day. What's that all about? Under what circumstance would someone need to eat ice cream in the bathroom? It's not just that they are sloppy kids. It's just that come summertime, they turn into horrible roommates.

I have been training these kids to be tidy cooperators since they were two years old. The lessons to flush, rinse and pick up after themselves should be deeply entrenched in their psyche by now. You would think. But something about summer makes my little lovelies act like they are on a Carnival Cruise Ship and I am the cabin attendant. No wonder Mommy's on the warpath.

Now, if I ever turned my laptop over to my children, no doubt a different story would emerge. They have told me multiple times that they do more chores than the rest of the neighbor's kids combined. "You'll thank me one day, " I crow. Recently, a friend came to visit with her husband and four children in tow. The conversation turned to a chore comparison.

"Do you guys do the dishes? Vacuum? Dust? Do your own laundry?" my kids asked hers. They answered every query to the negative.

"No way!" they said confidently. "Our mother does all that at our house."

"Not here!" My child responded. "We do everything! Our parents don't do anything."

Keep laughing. Just be warned. If you want to use the bathroom at our house during the summer, you should bring your own paper. It's true that for nine months of the year, there is some semblance of order around here. I think it's because when they are in school, I expect to do more than my fair share. But when they are on the computer playing World of Warcraft for six hours a day, I don't think a roll replacement is asking too much. If they would just put some of the effort they pour into their Facebook pages, we'd all get along just fine. I'm asking you....is a little summer help asking too much?

I am inspired to keep training these Byrds to keep their nests tidy. You see, I don't want them to turn out like my friend Beckie. Beckie never had to do any chores while growing up. She went to college and graduated, chore-free. While living in her first apartment, Beckie was horrified to find black mold growing in her toilet. She called the Water Department in her town and told them there was something wrong with her water. She demanded they come and fix it. After a series of questions, they deduced the real problem.

"Ma'am, have you cleaned your toilet lately?" they inquired. The Water Department Supervisor then went on to describe to Beckie how to properly and frequently clean her toilet so black mold wouldn't grow.

This story has been my inspiration. I may yell, cajole, insult and even drip-dry, but by golly, these kids will learn how to be consummate toilet-cleaners before they leave my house. Just give me a few more years with them and they'll learn their role regarding rolls. By then, auto-refill, auto-flush toilets should hit the home market. Sigh…heaven.

Is Mom the Tooth Fairy?

"Do you believe in God?" I asked one of my teens this summer. "I don't get it *all*..." Alex answered slowly, "It doesn't *all* make sense to me."

Oh baby, welcome to the club. I cherish the honesty in that statement. Who, after all, does "get it all"? People who say they understand it *all* scare me. They're just a little too RIGHT, if you know what I mean. (Dana Carvey as the Church Lady on Saturday Night Live always comes to mind.)

We don't need to "get it all." We never will. We're only asked to have child-like faith. Children believe in things without first-hand evidence. They believe simply because they want to believe. No proof required.

Something sad happens as we age, however. Our skepticism grows and grows. We start to require proof. We demand answers and explanations. Like this letter that was left on my bedside table recently,

"Mom, why do you/ the tooth fairy always give me 50 cents. Can I have a dollar or two?"

Skeptism drizzled off the page. Who leaves me money? Is it Mom? Or is it the tooth fairy? Why is she so cheap? Mom is cheap. That might mean Mom is the tooth fairy. That settles it. My mom is the tooth fairy. (Note: we never once told our kids there was a tooth fairy, we simply left them a paltry few coins to celebrate the new hole in their mouth.)

We want to know...is this real or isn't it? Parents, seeking to be imaginative and cute, muddy the pure water of our children's believing hearts. They're just not sure what to believe. Early on, Dave and I committed to always telling our kids the truth and nothin' but the truth. To my knowledge, I only slipped once. But it was a biggie.

When my kids were little, they wanted to know what happened to their baby teeth after they fell out. I made up a fairy tale in which their tiny little teeth were dropped into the ocean and grew into beautiful pearls. In reality, I flushed them down the toilet. Who knows? They say all paths lead to the ocean...they could have become pearls. However, as you might have noticed, this was not the whole truth. It came back to haunt me.

Trevor was born skeptical. He decided to test the pearl theory. He set out to grow a pearl in his bedroom. I tried to stop him by explaining that it wasn't the ocean. He simply added some salt to the water. He saved a tooth, put it in a jar in his bedroom, and watched it every day, waiting for the transformation. All he learned is that Mommy tells tall tales or is perhaps a big fat liar. Plus we all learned that a tooth in water starts to really stink over time.

Trevor is my own personal Doubting Thomas. Doubting Thomas got the bum rap in Scripture because he demanded proof. He was out of the room when Christ came back from the dead. He didn't believe his friends when they told him about it. He said he'd need to see --and feel! -- for himself. I can relate. So can Trevor. Asking for something to go on isn't such a bad thing, really. God understands.

When Jesus came in through the walls, he said, "Peace be with you!" It's the equivalent of saying, "Relax." Or maybe even "Chill." He did not take the time to explain how he came in without opening the door. It was information they didn't need to know. Just relax. And believe. You'll be blessed. He is one cool dude.

Blessed are those who have not seen and yet have believed. I think Jesus purposely didn't explain every little thing. If we knew it all, we wouldn't need faith. Faith is believing what we do not see. We don't have to have all the answers. We can come to the Lord with the tiniest smidgen of faith. We can say, "Are you the Lord, or aren't you?" He's delighted to enter into the Grand Conversation with us.

So, as I say to my Alex, "You don't have to understand it all, honey. Stop doubting and believe." And Julia, I'm glad you asked. Yes, Julia, your mom is the tooth fairy at our house and fifty cents is all you'll ever get for a tooth.

Laptop for Dummies

Dave bought me a laptop the other day. "My wife's a writer," he told the kid at Best Buy. He was too stoned or hung-over to appear impressed. (The kid, that is, not Dave.)

At Circuit City, they asked what we'd use the laptop for.

Dave replied, "Writing." It sounded thrilling and very, very official.

He bought all the bells and whistles for me...the additional keyboard, the docking station. The docking, I gather, is so I don't mess up the laptop when I bring it back home from an outing. It's simple. Laptop for Dummies. At least, it's meant to be.

The first day I decided to take the laptop out of the house, I had to ask my technical support guy, Trevor, to unplug and bag it up for me.

"Don't you want to take the plastic off, Mom?" He inquired, peeling its protective covering back. "No!" I shouted. "I don't want it to get fingerprints!" He rolled his eyes so far back in his head that they almost got stuck.

It's a shiny black laptop. The cover is so shiny black it would be awesome if it was involved in a crime because the perps' fingerprints would show up clearly on the lacquered finish. (Too much Law & Order, you think?)

"I'm going to leave that on," I lamely explained. I want it to stay shiny.

Biting his tongue, Trevor undocked it, fastened it safely in the computer bag and put it in my car.

When I got to Panera Bread, I was feelin' fine. I was looking professional-ish, carrying my laptop bag. At that time of morning, there are business people getting their coffees and taking their meetings and there was me, blending in. I could have passed for one of them. Or so I imagined.

I got to the table while imagining that others were admiring me and my laptop bag. I put the shiny laptop on the table with is glorious hp logo facing me and its shiny packaging cling screen capturing the light. I reached to open it and start my fantastic writing career when…

It wouldn't open. I pressed repeatedly on the two buttons that were facing me. They appeared to be keeping the laptop tightly closed. I discreetly felt my way around the edges, looking for a magic latch.

Now, I glanced around hoping no one was watching me. I wasn't too worried about being embarrassed. I just didn't want anyone to think I was in possession of a stolen laptop. It was clearly new (cling strip.) Could it have been lifted from PC World? After all, who can't open their very own laptop?

As I do in all times of despair, I said a prayer over the laptop, leaving my fingerprints on it as I laid holy hands on it in prayer. Dear God, help me to open my laptop in Jesus' name, Amen. I tried again. I pressed on those buttons. Nothing. Nada. It didn't budge.

I looked at all the edges of the laptop and saw, to my chagrin and relief, a small spot for a key.

"Trevor must have locked it!" I figured. "And the key is, of course, at home!" Humbled and saddened, I slid my prized laptop back in the bag. It would go home, unscathed.

Later that day my friend Joy was using the same model laptop. Well, nearly the same. Hers was white and she had thrown the protective plastic covering away. (But it was white…no crime scene fingerprints!).

"How do you open your laptop?" I begged her for wisdom.

She flipped it open with ease.

"Gosh, mine doesn't do that," I said, "It has some type of lock on it." She looked at me quizzically but didn't say anything. Her expression said "Gee, they'll let anyone with $799 buy one of those things, won't they?"

Delivering my laptop safely back to the docking station at home, I waited for Trevor to return from school.

"How'd you do with the laptop?" he asked excitedly.

"It was locked. You must have locked it," I accused Tech Support.

"Huh?" he asked as he easily flipped open the screen with a single finger.

I had it backwards.
I was trying to open it by the hinges.
It was that logo that faked me out.
That and my peri-menopausal brain.

All I can surmise is that God wanted me to use paper and pen that morning at Panera. And to get over myself.

Yes, get over myself.

I am fully convinced that it's only because I thought I was So Cool, Mrs. All-That-and-Then-Some, that my laptop wouldn't open.

Pride goes before a fall.   And before a laptop, too, I guess.

In Defense of Bad Language

Sure, most people agree that crap is a four-letter word, but is it a swear word? This is a discussion that we've been having around our house for a number of years. Back when the kids were young, I can remember discussing it with my friends Debi and Angela. Debi and I both said crap with some regularity; Angela did not. Debi and I concluded it would be an acceptable swear-substitute; Angela did not. Guess whose kids are allowed to say crap?

Is there even such a thing as a swear-substitute? I ponder these weighty questions late at night when I can't sleep. Caroline came home from her Christian school with a list of forbidden words. The list was made up of mostly swear-substitutes. "You can't say "darn" because it's a form of the other "d" word," she informed us. I pretended I didn't know what the other "d word" was, testing her out, but she passed. She didn't say the other "d word". She just rolled her eyes at me and continued on.

"You can't say "shoot" because it's a substitute for the other "s" word."

"You can't say "heck" because it's a substitute for the other "h" word."

"You can't say drat, for the same reason you can't say darn."

Can you say, "Oh boy?!" I interjected. She was not amused.

It made me wonder. I personally always favored the swear-substitute. I had no idea that a swear –substitute was just as bad as a swear. (Is it? This is the question that I'm wrestling with.) I know the Bible says, "Let no unwholesome talk come out of your mouth." That is certainly a broad enough road to walk on. But what I consider wholesome someone else may consider unwholesome. I've had whole interventions done on me over my liberal use of the word 'crap'. In fact, this chapter will probably have to be cut from the book if I want nice people to read it without taking offense.

I've let one or two swear words fly from my wholesome lips over the past year or two. Generally I do this when in heated conversations with my teenage sons. I know that it will get their attention and let them know without a doubt just how hot under the collar I am at that moment. I'm not exactly Howard Stern, and I'm not referring to the f-bomb here, but I do think that when I say something that I don't normally say, people stop and listen.

It's like an EF Hutton moment, and I'm frankly unwilling to give it up unless the Lord himself tells me I have to. Case in point, I let one fly just yesterday. My twin sister Carey said, "Did you just say….? You never say that!" I triumphed, "That's right, didn't it make my point exactly?" She had to conclude the word did indeed punctuate my sentence in an unexpected way. She will never forget what I said now.

Swear-substitutes are pretty subjective, too. According to some, you can't say "golly" or "gee" as these are taking the Lord's name in vain. If you didn't catch on (like I didn't), the fact that these words start with a "g" make them a God-substitute. Really? For real? That's where I draw the line. I've never once started my prayer, "Oh Gee" or "Oh holy Golly." Not even one time.

To see where my children stand on this issue, I just let fly the whole forbidden list. I called out: "Darn! Gosh! Golly! Shoot! Gee Whiz! Oh my gravy! Crap!"

Julia finally interrupted me to say, "Job jar!" Swearing is against our house rules and requires a trip to the job jar to receive a penalty task. I'm not sure what I said that tripped her off, actually. Crap! I really didn't want to do a chore today.

'Tis the Season (Bah Humbug)

'Tis the season for moms to pluck themselves bald, cry in the bathroom, pay extra for overnight delivery and oh yes, be jolly!

Kids get really greedy as the holidays approach. We teach them to be this way. When they are little we ask, "What do you want for Christmas?" and then we stupidly give it to them. Warning: As They Grow, So Does Their List of Demands.

I remember when my five were little. They loved toy catalogs. Pouring over these advertising rags, they would find themselves longing for items previously unknown. We were dumb. We bought them! That's how we ended up with a Snoopy Slushy Maker, a Gooey Bake Oven that made slimy creatures and my favorite, A Spy Set with real fingerprinting kit. These things made a splash on Christmas morning but left our house by January after they rapidly broke, burned little hands or, in the case of the fingerprinting kit, ruined the bedroom carpet.

9-year-old Julia is only limited by her imagination. Last week she blissfully circled items from the Lands' End catalog. She doesn't need clothes; she has more clothes than Barbie. She circled the three puppies on the cover. To make sure I understood, she wrote in the margin, "THE DOGS."

I have told her before that Santa can't carry live creatures in his sleigh. But she is not deterred. She turned to the infant section and circled the babies. In the margin, she wrote, "BABIES!" Now that she's in fourth grade, she's ready to be a mother. Warning to parents with small kids: Do Not Give Them What They Want. I've seen where that leads and believe me, it's not pretty!

When they are little and they make a Christmas list, we think it's adorable. We meet their wants because we can, and their top request costs $9.99. As they grow, beware, so do their desires. Last year my niece Rebecca asked for a giraffe that reaches the sky. My sister made a fatal flaw. She gave it to her. She searched the world and found a six-foot tall stuffed giraffe. What will Rebecca want when she's a teen? An African Safari?

What do the teens want? Whatever is new and crazy-expensive. Last year's model of anything is idiotic. If they have Xbox, it's dumb. They want Xbox 360. If they have an iPod mini, it's a piece of junk. They want a video iPod. Just the batteries and rechargers for the electronics cost more than we're willing to spend!

Now, the boys favor the Best Buy catalog. We're sunk, because they are no longer satisfied with action figures or wooden blocks. No, the things they want cost a fortune. And we don't even have the satisfaction of surprising them on Christmas morning.

My boys are master spies (due, no doubt, to that kit that ruined the carpet.) Old enough to know better, they still sneak around, trying to see their gifts before Christmas. They immorally rip into wrapped gifts to see what they are. Without shame, they'll even say, "Mom, some of these packages got ripped under the tree!"

We have neither the cash nor the desire to purchase the wow factor gifts like convertibles and flat screen TVs for their rooms. All we have on our side is the element of surprise. And that's been taken from us over the last few years. They are just too impatient! So here's what I'm going to do this year. *(Byrd kids, stop reading here, or your entire Christmas will be ruined.)*

I'm just not going to get them anything. Now that will be a surprise!

This will accomplish several objectives.

One, I will not be crazed running from store to store, trying to make dreams come true.
Two, I will save lots and lots of money.
Three, I will keep all my hair.
Four, I will not have to watch in frustration as they update their

lists until Christmas Eve.
Five, I will have nothing to hide in my closet.
Six, I will have nothing to wrap.
Seven, I will not have to stand in line returning things they claimed they really wanted.
Eight, I will not have to get a puppy or have a baby!
Nine, I will be able to see my charge bill in January without first taking a tranquilizer.
Ten, I will enjoy the holidays this year.

What do you think?

(I know the kids are still reading and note to Byrd kids: I am NOT KIDDING!).

This year, my kids are getting stockings, empty even of coal. When the UPS man comes to deliver the giraffe, I won't answer the door. No Guitar Hero 3. No new cell phones. No refrigerator for his bedroom (a real request, by the way.) And I'm still not kidding. Happy Holidays, everyone. Bah humbug!

Puppy Love

Can you imagine being a teenager and having your mom write something called "Puppy Love"? Would you just run away from home or what? That's why, just for a few pages, I will not use my own teens as examples. Some things are just too sacred. Puppy love is crazy, spastic and unreasonable. No kid wants their mom talking about it in public.

What is Puppy Love? For those who have totally blocked out adolescence, I Googled the definition and here's what I got:

Puppy love is an informal term for feelings of love, particularly between young people during adolescence, so-called for its resemblance to the adoring, worshipful affection that may be felt by a puppy.

Now that we are old enough to know better (or so we tell our kids), we can see how foolish Puppy Love is. Sure, <u>now</u> we think unrequited teen crushes are a waste of time. But back then…ah, it was more real than homework, more real than chores, more real than your favorite TV show. Puppy Love is all-consuming, but kids, take it from your Aunt Martie, you'll be embarrassed by it one day. Maybe even tomorrow.

What drives young people to have this depth of passion that's so undeserved and unreciprocated? Why do young girls hang posters Zac Efron from *High School Musical* in their rooms? They speak reverently about this guy and sacrifice a week's allowance to buy the Disney magazine. Yes, okay, I did it, too. Is Tiger Beat still in print? But give me a break, kids. His voice still cracks!

Girls! Boys! There is plenty of time for this foolishness later on, when your brains are fully developed. Scientists say that will be in your mid-twenties. Still, I shouldn't really scold. I remember my own personal Zac Efron. His name was Jorge Rodriguez. I spotted him during public skate at a rink in my hometown. His dark curly locks, his way of completely ignoring me….SIGH! November 27, 1977. The day I first saw Jorge. I committed it to memory. Twenty-seven became my favorite number, which has endured to this day. (In a God-has-a-sense-of-humor-moment, guess the date I met my husband? November 27! It's a magical date. But back to Jorge.)

Throughout high school, I called his house and hung up immediately after hearing his adolescent voice saying, "Hello? Hello?" Occasionally, I also got to hear the voice of his irate mother saying, "If you don't stop doing this, I'm going to call the police." Ah, puppy love.

Whatever happened to Jorge? His parents moved him out of town and thus ruined my life. Did I mention he never even spoke to me? Where is he now? Hold on while I Google his name.

Oh my gosh, you will absolutely not believe it. Jorge Rodriguez is famous. I knew it! I knew he was special! He's in Hollywood. He has tons of movies to his credit. He's most recently worked on a children's movie. I will drag my children to see it and clap when I see his name. My heart is pounding.

But imagine my crushing disappointment; no photo available. Slim biological information. No mention of our hometown in Connecticut. No mention of me at all!

And was his middle initial "C"? Because this movie guy is Jorge C. Rodriguez. But I just feel in my heart it's my guy. A woman knows these things.

I clicked on a fan site called "Who's Dated Who." It would allow me to upload a picture of Jorge and give stats on who he's dated. While it's a bit of a stretch to say we actually dated, he did walk by my house once during a snow storm. I consider posting.

I do have a picture of him. Where's the 1978 yearbook? Okay, yes, so the only picture I have of him is from my Junior High yearbook. I could still send it in. Do they take pictures with a heart drawn around it in marker?

I'm remembering how Puppy Love felt. These days we call it stalking and there are laws against it. I called my twin sister Carey and said, "Do you remember Jorge Rodriguez's middle initial?" (Everyone in my family remembers Jorge.)

She said, "It's C."

I knew it, knew it, knew it. I knew he would be famous. Should I contact him? Just to wish him well and ask how his mother is doing? He'd probably like to see a picture of my kids, don't you think? On a whim I did send him a Friend Request on Facebook. Just like in the seventies, he didn't respond to me. Flashing back to Junior High, I considered sending him seventy-five more requests and forcing him to acknowledge my presence. Sigh.

And that's what Puppy Love is like.   Sick.

Torture at a Middle School Dance

Recently, I was driving down the highway with my van full of teens when a scary thing happened. The opening bars of Stairway to Heaven played on our car radio, and I broke into a cold sweat. "Turn it off! Wait, I changed my mind! Turn it up!" I shouted. The kids looked at me as if I was a lunatic. Little did they know I was being transported back thirty years, to the gym of my junior high school. Stairway to Heaven was the song that was always played during a slow dance.

For me, it's still not a happy song. In eighth grade I had thick glasses, shiny braces, and was the personification of awkward. I wasn't going out with anyone in those days, but hope sprung eternal when the school dances were announced. Maybe, just maybe, someone would ask me to slow dance.

In preparation for the Big Show, my friends and I would spend hours preparing. In particular I remember we soaked ourselves in Love's Baby Soft body spray and smelled each other's breath to make sure it was minty fresh. Just the perfect casual outfit had to be selected. You know, the one that says, "This old thing? I just threw this together at the last minute" even though we had spent hours trying and rejecting every single outfit we owned. All this preparation, leading up to a few hours in the school gym.

I'm serious; lives were made and ruined in that place. Now, to enhance my already awkward appearance and uncool clothes, I made a radical decision. Although I am legally blind and can't see six inches in front of my face, I would leave my glasses at home the night of the dance. This way, I was sure that hunks would be knocked over with my previously unrecognized beauty. (Most of my favorite movies have this exact plot.)

Blind, I'd memorize the colors of my friends' outfits and ask them to describe what my current crush was wearing. Like a baby gosling imprinting on a mother goose, I could only follow blurry patches of color. If my friends left me alone, I was sunk. I couldn't see a thing! I would have to sit on the bleachers until someone came to rescue me.

The place to avoid during a school dance was the bathroom. The smoking didn't bother me as much as the crying. The bathroom was Heartbreak Hotel. It was the place of refuge for girls fighting with their boyfriends, breaking up the night of the dance or those who were not asked to dance. Emotions ran high in the Girl's Room.

Back to Stairway to Heaven. For one, it's possibly the longest song ever to be recorded. Okay, it's actually about eight minutes long. But, if you add adolescent angst to it, it's easily forty-five minutes long. Just the introduction is over two minutes long. Yet someone may, just may, ask you to dance during the opening bars. This gives plenty of time for hope to die a painful death.

"Maybe he just can't see where I am standing."

"Maybe he's not wearing his glasses."

"Maybe he's checking his breath in the bathroom."

"Maybe he doesn't recognize me because I look so good tonight."

And finally, "Maybe he asked someone else."

If a girl is asked to dance, she has the opportunity to say yes, no matter who asks. She can just be relieved to not sit it out with me on the bleachers. Or, she can throw caution to the wind, say no, and keep her options open for the cute guy from French class to come over and ask her. If she says no, she hasn't taken the Stairway to Heaven. She's taken the Hallway to the Bathroom. The Walk of Shame.

Now, don't feel too sorry for me. I did get asked to dance a time or two during those years. And let me tell you, dear friends, I don't believe Led Zeppelin was thinking of slow dancers when they penned Stairway to Heaven. It may be universally recognized as one of the greatest rock songs of all time, but it's really hard to dance to! It starts slow, but ends with some rock, and what exactly are dancers supposed to do? The real couple clung to each other during the fast parts. Cheaper than a drive in, I guess. Sometimes it appeared they couldn't tell when the music stopped. But what about me dancing with Matt from my Confirmation Class at Church? I am blushing just thinking of it. Awkward, awkward song.

Now my kids are old enough to go to school dances and I pray they have good memories. To my young readers, I offer you these words of hope. Try not to cry. Laugh, instead. And don't worry so much about your outfits. You'll never remember what you wore, but you'll never forget the songs.

Takin' Our Show on the Road

Our family of seven isn't invited too many places. Those who invite us to stay at their homes can be:

a) Instantly nominated for sainthood
b) Listed on the fingers of one hand
c) Seen calling Stanley Steamer as our van pulls away
d) All of the above.

It's not that we mean to be a traveling catastrophe. That's just the way we roll. Once a year or so, we leave Virginia for a New England Odyssey to visit family and friends. This consists of us spending one or two nights in each of three or four states, and driving through every New England state except for Maine. Now, doesn't that sound like fun??

When the kids were smaller, we thought we had it rough because we had to pack diapers and bottles and their itty bitty clothing. We'd strap the kids in their seats and off we'd go. What was so hard about that? Now, all of our children are adult-sized except for Julia. Being the little one, she gets crammed in the back, between two man-sized brothers for most trips…and usually ends up crying at some point. Who can blame her?

Our seven-passenger van is ridiculously small to hold both our family and our luggage. Heading off with our brood is akin to fitting a bunch of clowns in a VW Bug. To make more space in the car (without leaving kids at home!), we've tried various car toppers. We haven't had much luck. One car topper howled so badly that we all wanted to pluck ourselves bald by the end of the trip. The next car topper, the famed "Soft Pack," was mercifully quiet. It lay silently on top of the van, sucking all of the moisture out of the sky. When we arrived at our destination, oh, how delighted we were to find that all of our duffels, pillows and sleeping bags were drenched. Our entire visit to Grammy and Grandpa involved bringing our wet items to the Laundromat. Can you say "family fun"?

Everyone wants to be comfortable on a trip. When the kids were little, their comfort came in the form of a little lovey object, like a stuffed animal or a baby blanket. Now, comfort has hit the Big Time. We begin with ten pillows and five blankets so no one is forced to share. Then we add a cooler, snacks, iPods, headphones, Game boys, games, chargers, cell phones, books, schoolwork that never gets touched but likes to go traveling and our two specialty totes. One tote holds all of our cosmetic bags or ditty bags as we lovingly call them. The other large tote is for shoes.

On an average trip, we will carry fourteen pairs of shoes. If there is going to be a dressy occasion, add seven pairs. Recently, in a desperate attempt to simplify, I assigned the dress shoes their own tote bag. You can probably see the simple genius in that idea, right?

On the Odyssey, we had a small near-catastrophe which involved putting a cheap plastic suitcase next to a burning hot radiator in a lovely bed and breakfast. The suitcase melted all over Caroline's clothes. We were horrified at the scorched remains. It was close to a real fire and we were grateful that it did not break out. Dave and I were pretty shaken.

We salvaged what we could and tossed the suitcase which Caroline had gotten for her birthday. Caroline was also pretty traumatized (she's no dummy), so I went into crises management mode in an effort to gloss over and move on. Casting about for a new suitcase for her, eyes lit upon the dress shoe tote. Lickety-split we emptied it of shoes and made it the new suitcase. She was satisfied with the solution. The dress shoes would have to travel home in a kitchen trash bag.

Because we try our level best to be nice guests, we always sweep, strip the beds, wipe the bathroom counters and of course, take out the trash. We do this because it's the right thing to do, and also so that if we aren't invited back, we can be sure it wasn't because we trashed the joint. We did all this tidying up before leaving the Melting Suitcase Inn. We moved briskly and we able to head to our next destination on time. No harm, no foul. Or so we thought.

A month later, the boys and Caroline were required to dress up for school one day. A Dress Up day requires leather shoes for the boys. It only comes a few times a year but they always groan and complain about it. In the midst of their groaning this time, they realized that they hadn't seen their dress shoes in quite some time.

They played "When was the last time you saw your shoes?" It didn't take long for the winning answer. You guessed it; the last time we had seen our dress shoes was at the Melting Suitcase Inn. In our frenzy to clean spic and span, one of our fabulous helpers took out an extra trash bag. That's how all of our dress shoes ended up in a dumpster in Massachusetts.

You can clearly see that traveling with our five teenagers is a total laugh riot. But all the wet luggage, tossed shoes and singed luggage is worth it to spend time with friends and family. We are open to any and all invitations so don't hesitate to ask! Seriously, we are tidy and we hardly ever start fires. Really.

Personal Style

Each Byrd in my family has his or her own personal style. This causes us to clash horribly in family pictures. This was never more evident than my father's 80th birthday party. Together, we sported at least eight different patterns. Yes, I knew there would be pictures taken. No, I couldn't make us match. All the other families looked coordinated, like the LL Bean catalog. My twin sister Carey's family was the best. Her husband and sons all wore blue oxfords. She and her daughter wore red dresses. They were Picture Perfect.

Then there's us. I do know what looks good in a photograph. I'm just too exhausted to battle my kids to wear it. There, I've said it. I'm tired of fighting my kids. They don't feel like matching. They don't feel like wearing oxfords. They each march to the beat of their own drummers and I let 'em. That's how we end up looking the way we do.

Who am I kidding, anyway? I gave up the fight years ago. That fifth child pushed me over the edge. Church members snickered when our toddler Julia attended services wearing a Tinker bell costume and mismatched plastic shoes from the Dollar Tree. If you want cute and matching kids, only have two.

Jackie O. never wore anything patterned. No kidding, never. There's only one picture of her in a print dress and it's a famous shot because it's so uncharacteristic. When I read that, I didn't wear patterns for years. Then I realized that:

a) I'm not Jackie O.
b) I like patterns.

They draw the attention away from my figure flaws...or so I imagine. Perhaps in analyzing our family photo, you'd draw a different conclusion.

At age sixteen Alex has one night shirt. It's blue. He wears it for every special occasion. Dance at school? Blue shirt. Family reunion? Blue shirt. Funeral, Christmas day, job interview? Blue shirt. (Just kidding about the job interview...for those he wears a skull shirt and never gets the job.)

At age fourteen Daniel considers hair his most important fashion accessory. His goal is to never show his eyes. He told me the reason he grows his hair is because he doesn't want to wear sunglasses. He mutes bright sunshine through a curtain of his own golden locks. To offset the Surfer Boy hair, he wears black. All black. For my dad's party, I begged him not to wear the *Nightmare Before Christmas* belt buckle that gives me an ulcer. Trevor also wears black. They are like twin Johnny Cash impersonators, except they are blonde and don't know who Johnny Cash is. I'm hoping they outgrow it.

Aged nine, Julia weighs fifty-four pounds. She is forever weighing herself. She pretends to not like her pencil-thin physique, but dresses to highlight her flatness. Trying on dresses recently, she rejected all the ones that swung away from her body. I call her the Human Bratz Doll. She does not follow fashion; she sets it. She is my fashion advisor. I can't wait to see how she turns out. If she starts wearing black every day, I'll cry.

This particular event inspired tweenaged Caroline to willingly don her first dress. From ages six through ten, she refused. She was strictly Old Navy, all the way. So, for her to wear a dress...big deal. Big, big deal. Proper-undergarments-and-stockings-kind-of-deal. First-pair-of-high-heels-deal. Make-her-dad-cry-she-looks-so-grown-up-deal. She is beautiful. And she still likes me.

I recently read that cancer-battling ex-presidential candidate's wife Elizabeth Edwards is writing letters to her children full of advice for their futures. She writes, "Never wear patterns. You'll regret them every time you see a photograph." Has she been looking at my family photo albums? Or reading a biography of Jackie O? Should I give similar advice to my kids?

Nah. Let them figure it out for themselves. I like patterns in pictures. You can easily see what decade it was. Some of the greatest commemorative family shots feature horrible prints from the 60's and 70's. How boring life would be if we wore navy blue all the time. How could we tell what year it was?

In allowing my brood to pick their own outfits, I am giving them the gift of future laughs. I'm giving them the confidence to choose their own style…good, bad or ugly. That's something, right? Personal style reflects on them….not me. At least that is what I keep telling myself.

Wii are Family

I love games. Scrabble, Yahtzee, Monopoly, I love 'em. Frequently I chase my family members around the house saying, *"Wanna play a game?"* Or the more challenging, *"Want me to whup you at Battleship?"* Sadly, no one really shares my love of board games. Despite their reluctance, I keep trying to plant seeds of board game love. We have a full game closet and a family room dripping with games, yet we get several new additions each year. This year, Julia got The Game of Life and Alex got Apples to Apples. We've played each game once. You see, there's a new sheriff in town. The video game.

65% of American families play video or computer games. Although I tried for years to not be a part of that statistic, we succumbed. Well, Dave did. I had highfalutin' opinions about how game systems are proven to give kids ADD while turning their brains to jello and ruining their chance of higher education or future happiness. Still, my darling husband Dave bought our first system, N64, about 10 years ago. He snuck it in the house late one Saturday night in the spring. The next morning, he blithely blamed it on the Easter Bunny.

Once that first system arrived, they kept coming. Sort of like the kids. You see, once we had one system, we wanted another one. We loved it just that much. I asked the kids to list these boxes that have lived in our home. Apparently, after the N64, we've owned GameCubes, Playstation 2s, an Xbox, and the stunner that arrived this Christmas, the Wii. Here's the problem. Once you buy a system, you need the controllers, the games and all the cool accessories. Then, moments after you're done purchasing everything you need, your friends procure the next, far better system (so they claim), and voila! Your system is passé. In order to keep up with the neighbors (as well as keep the kids *plugged in* instead of riding bikes or reading the classics), you've got to keep buying more stuff. Frankly, it only took four minutes before I was sick of the whole mess.

Once our clever Alex wanted to offload his GameCube in order to purchase another system. Being a 21st century kid, he naturally offered his GameCube for sale on eBay. The whole family was excited as we watched the bids mount. He was only twelve years old and since the system was a gift to him, he was looking at pure profit from the sale. Then we ran into a snag. An interested party posted an inquiry asking if he had any games that went along with the system.

He answered, *"I can throw a few in."* While this sounds suave and all, his mother nearly swallowed her tongue. The games run about $50 a pop, so selling the system for $100 would mean zero profit if he "threw in" two games. I did what any mom would do. I started bidding against this woman, seeking to drive up the price. It was working great, really great. The price was going up and up and up. Until, in my greed, with less than a minute to spare, I bid one last time…and inadvertently won the bid.

"MOM!" Alex groaned at top volume, "You just bought my GameCube!"

Oops. Until recently, that eBay debacle was the only time I had anything to do with a game system in our house. That is, until this Christmas. You see, this year our generous "Santa Dan" gifted us with the Wii entertainment system and all the cool accessories. Thanks, Santa Dan! Thanks, Aunt Janet! Wii fell in love with it. Yes, even Mii. I was hooked from the early moments of Christmas day.

The first thing you do is make a little Mii character that is your avatar on the game. You should see how tall, thin and fresh-faced my avatar is! She doesn't have a single wrinkle! She looks just like me twenty-five years ago. And you should see her bowling! Okay, well, she bowls like she's playing softball, but she doesn't have wrinkles and never yells at her kids or goes out without lipstick.

Wii are now so cool. Wii have joined with the fifty million others who have welcomed their own darling Wii to their family room. Since Wii have welcomed our Wii, everyone wants to play a game with Mom. Or Dad. Or the cats. They'll play with anyone who can swing the remote, pretending it's a golf club, a tennis racquet or a bowling ball. It's the most exercise we've gotten together in years. What differentiates Wii from the other systems we've had? In a word, fun. This system is one that everyone (even Mom!) can play.

Dad loves it, too. He's joined the 26% of gamers who are over fifty. Great news! Video games are now becoming popular in nursing homes! He'll be all set! When asked what it's like to play with Dad on the Wii, here are some of the comments from his five adoring children.

"He gets really mad."
"He doesn't understand how to swing it."
"Then he growls…aaaagggrrrrr!"
"He loves it when he's winning and hates it when he is losing."

Now, doesn't that sound like family time at its greatest??? That's why I say, with pride (and only a little chagrin), "Wii are family."

Makin' the Grade

Back in the seventies and eighties, when I was in school, kids did their own homework and parents watched the evening news while enjoying adult conversation, a cocktail and a bowl of dry roasted peanuts. I never dreamed of asking my parents to help me make a papier-mache volcano that actually erupted. Instead, I made projects the old-fashioned way: with supplies found around the house or yard. We didn't have a craft drawer in our kitchen or a supply of Modge Podge in the cupboard. We didn't have twelve cans of metallic spray paint and flexible tubing in the garage. We had hangers, tissue paper and imagination. In short, we just made it work.

That was then, this is now. As a parent, I have found to my horror that these days, parents are considered something like co-students. It took me several years of Back to School Nights before I caught on. At first, I just thought that the science projects on display indicated that the students at our schools were extraordinarily gifted. *"I can't believe that a <u>child</u> made this from his Erector set!"* Guess what? They didn't.

As a traditionalist, I refused to help my kids. For years they suffered under my Sink or Swim regime. Last year, I did concede that there was a pressing need for poster board in our home. I bought it in bulk. Unfortunately, instead of using it for school, my girls started a series of lemonade stands and advertised with handmade signs. My favorite was when their stand went sugar-free. Then the sign read "Ice Cold Water." They made $11.75. Talk about ingenuity!

As a long-time parent of a lot of kids, I agree with Solomon in the Bible. There really is nothing new under the sun. Life with my fifth 5th grader is like watching the movie *Groundhog Day*. You know, it's the one where Bill Murray is forced to relive the same day over and over again. Been there, done that. Ask me anything. Mountain ranges in the United States? Check. Spelling Words? Yawn. Life cycle of a butterfly? Snore. Now mind you, I'm not implying I'm in any way smarter than a fifth grader. I'm just saying this is now my sixth time through the grade. I ought to know my way around by now.

Now, my high school students are certainly too cool to ask for my help or even pause a second to listen to my sage advice. Yet having seen some killer projects in my day, I'm compelled to make some suggestions. They run for the hills when they have a project involving sales or marketing. With my background in advertising, I can't let an opportunity like that pass. If they want to run for student government, I want to come up with the world's best slogan. These children of mine reject all my ideas. *"But I almost won a Clio for Excellence in Advertising!"* I say, as I chase them around with my list of clever headlines.

To help or not to help? That is the question. Clearly by the time they are teens, they should be doing most things for themselves. By age sixteen they should have a debit card, their own method for treating laundry stains, and they should be able to complete their own schoolwork. Yet the competitive nature of college admission, coupled with a big dose of *"What is everyone else doing?"* makes even the most reluctant parent start to worry.

"Have you finished your homework?" is repeated so often in my home that I'm thinking of recording it on a microchip to avoid straining my voice. If they say yes, I follow it up with the clincher, *"Have you done everything you can do to be a successful student today?"* This question never garners a yes; instead the teens grit their teeth and storm up to their rooms to listen to their iPods while pretending to be cramming for exams.

Recently, our final fifth grader, our gorgeous Julia, had a volcano project to do. Guys, I couldn't help myself. I bought tissue paper, got out the Modge Podge, and jumped right in. It's going to actually explode when yeast is added to a water bottle filled with peroxide and get this: the foam will be red! We used the paint that I keep stored in the craft drawer in the kitchen. I guess I've become a softy in my old age. I hope we, er, I mean she, gets an "A".

It's All Poop

We had a beautiful all-white house in Dallas, Texas. The walls were white, the molding was white, the carpet was white. I had three toddler boys in this house and I was a slave to the carpet and walls. I went nuts if someone tried to step off the kitchen floor with a juice cup.

"On the hard floor!" I would bellow. The kids were only allowed to drink their sippy cups on the tile floor. I had already learned that sippy cups are overrated. Either the valves leak or the milk cups get lost under a bed and start to stink or they drip sticky dew on my white rugs. The kids had to stay on the hard floor. I was just that clean.

We had one four-year old, two two-year olds and I was very pregnant with our fourth child. Seemed like a good time to try to sell the house. I was longing to move back East. Every day was about 112 degrees and I was convinced my brain was frying like an egg in my skull. Oh yes, and we were trying For Sale By Owner. I didn't have enough to do. Let's sell the house ourselves and save a few bucks; what a great idea!

One day, a couple came by unexpectedly wanting to take a quick peek. The extent of the devastation in our upstairs can only be compared to Hurricane Katrina. After they left, I actually went through and videotaped the mountains of laundry, unmade beds and unflushed toilets, wanting to document our shame for posterity. It was the day I realized that the realtors earn their commission simply by forcing people to make appointments for a showing.

These were the pre-potty-training days when the twins had a clever trick of taking each other's diapers off. They loved pulling the tape tabs off. They could not see past their own roly-poly toddler bellies to strip themselves but each had just the right skill set to free his brother from the confines of a

Pamper. We tried everything but potty training to break them of this habit. Duct tape around the perimeter of the diaper worked great. Too bad we hadn't duct-taped them into their soggy drawers on this fateful day.

So, this lovely young couple was looking at the house. They seemed a bit surprised about the upstairs and the fact that they couldn't see the carpet because every room was a trashed mess. They loved the kitchen, however, and perched there to discuss the particulars of the neighborhood, the electric bill and the like. These are major buying signals and Dave and I were excited. We finally had a hot prospect.

Just then the toddlers came charging through. Danny and Trevor parked themselves on the hard floor and started vying for attention. We did our best to swat them away. We needed all of our attention to fawn over the potential buyers. If we could sell the home ourselves, it would mean a hefty profit and we were already counting the money.

Ignoring the boys was a costly error. They knew just how to get out attention. Faster than you can say, "Oh crap!" one little guy denuded his twin of his steaming diaper.

Poop pellets showered out on the floor. And rolled.

I remember thinking hysterically that perhaps our buyers didn't notice. But then, sadly, one of the pellets landed just an inch from our buyer's shoe. I irrationally hoped that he would mistake it for a chocolate covered raisin as I calmly but swiftly scooped it up with a paper towel. As I stood up, however, I noticed the look of disgust and horror in his eyes. We finished up the conversation…I'm not sure why…as our business had just been concluded.

The house didn't sell for another six months. We had long since moved away to a shady house on the East Coast. We hired a good realtor. We learned our lesson. It goes something like this: "Don't sweat the small stuff. It's all poop."

I Found a Miracle in the Dryer

I found a miracle in my clothes dryer just now. It was my husband's wedding ring. It was clunking, clanking, rolling around in there but the dryer is always full of Legos, quarters and ballpoint pens, so I generally don't even check to see what's making the noise.

When I took the clothes out to fold them, the ring came popping out like some dramatic scene from the Lord of the Rings trilogy. The golden ring with etching of our anniversary so he would never forget...*My Precious*!

Here's the miracle. Dave's ring was rolling around in the dryer. I found it. I put it on and...*drum roll, please*...

I DID NOT EVEN FEEL ANGRY.

This is a bona fide miracle.

I didn't want to call him and chew him out.
I didn't want to call him and ask if he had a hot date.
I didn't want to call him and say, "Missing anything important?"

My husband always wears his ring. He likely took it off to lift weights this morning. He probably put it in the pocket of his gym shorts. This morning, being the good little wife that I am, I gathered up a load of dirty clothes just lying around. Really, let's be honest, I'm the one who washed his wedding ring.

God's the one who kept me from anger. Why is it such a miraculous thing? If you've been around me over the years, you wouldn't even have to ask that question. It's a miracle because it's truly a sign (or is that side effect?) that I am really being transformed. I'm a new me. It's just obvious by that reaction, or shall I say non-reaction. There's a Bible verse that says in Christ I am a new creation. It has a nice ring to it...especially when I start to see that it's actually true.

For so many years I would be mad/sad/tired/overworked and no matter what the situation, I would blame Dave. Irrational but true. One day I was rushing and frazzled. I threw bleach into a dark load of clothes in the washer. I got furiously angry at Dave and he wasn't even home at the time. Another time the car wouldn't start at the post office and I got mad at Dave. Once (well, much more than once), I was tired at the end of a long day and questioning if I was a good mother and if I could even survive until bedtime and, naturally…you guessed it……I got mad at Dave.

But this time, the burning hot ring came out of the dryer and I just put it on, no comment, no anger, no anything.

It's a miracle. And I'm grateful. I'm pretty sure Dave is grateful, too.

Teens, the New Toddlers

I worked at a preschool recently. After years of going stir crazy with tons of toddlers at home, I now have all big kids. They drive and shave and text. I actually missed having tiny people around. I love their butterfly kisses. I love decoding what they are trying to say. I like wiping their little hands before snack time and snuggling them with a blanky. My friend Amy said, "I think this will be an endorphin rush for you, sort of like breast feeding." I knew exactly what she meant and I agreed.

It was a great job. I loved the little people and found that I didn't mind the diapers or the runny noses or the fingers in my eyeballs again. I was surprised what I did find. For years I have looked back with regrets about how I acted when my kids were little. I remember being a mean, tired, distracted mom who needed timeouts on a regular basis. Through my preschool job, I was able to peek back into the world of toddlers and get a glimpse of how I acted. I liked what I saw.

I danced with the kids. I sang nursery rhymes. Who knew I remembered them? It was like riding a bike! I rolled their pudgy bellies into pizza dough, then "popped them in the oven and ate them all up!" I smiled and laughed and was never tired of stacking blocks so they could knock them all down again. I made up games and tickled and laughed. It was delightful.

I realized that these were well-practiced skills, games and techniques I was pulling up. I remembered! That was what I did at home when my five were small. I was delighted to become reacquainted with the old me. I felt a lot less guilty and a lot more competent. It was life-affirming and belly-laughing. I should have paid the preschool for letting me work there and find myself again.

The moms of toddlers were simply adorable. They sent in clean, happy and well-adjusted tiny tots to the Mother's Day Out program. They spoke with yearning for the days when their child would be potty-trained or out of preschool. I could see they were peering around the corner and sensing that Easy Street was just up ahead. If only they could pry the pacifier out of their child's teeth or get them to sleep through the night, they'd be all set.

Easy Street? I was aching to address their misperceptions, but didn't. I didn't because I knew they wouldn't believe me. I didn't believe older moms when I had small people. Why should they listen to me, the smiley lady who changes diapers and doles out Goldfish?

They all believed toddlerdom is a short walk on the way to Easy Street. If they could just live through the child's second or third year, they'd never traverse those halls again. Wrong, wrong, wrong. (See why I didn't say anything; I have no tact.) You see, teens are the new toddlers. If you don't get the upper hand during their toddler years, you'll have another opportunity. The same obstinate, obnoxious and selfish behaviors will revisit your home ten or twelve years from now. And the second time around, they have muscles and a mustache.

If you lose a verbal argument with a toddler, all is not lost. You simply pick him up and deposit him in his little toddler bed for a time out. If you lose an argument with a teenager, he may storm out into the neighborhood and may not come back for hours. Or he could grab the car keys. Or hop a bus to New York City.

If you don't like the dirty or stained shirt that your toddler insists on wearing, you just throw it away the next time it comes through the wash and that's the end of that. If a teen has such a shirt....he'll be sure to wear it every time you are trying to take a picture for the family Christmas card. He might wear it precisely because it bothers you.

If your toddler has the willpower to keep herself awake to spend time with mommy and daddy, you probably think it's sweet or bratty but either way you know it's because she wants more time with you. If your teenager stays up late, it's because she wants more time away from you.

I always resented the old ladies who said, "You just wait!" when I explained to them how my life would be easier just as soon as they were off the bottle or out of diapers or out of preschool. I still remember thinking we'd be financially secure as soon as we scratched diapers and formula off our grocery list. Sigh, those were the least expensive days we've ever had with our kids.

I'm sorry to be one of those old ladies, but this time you should really listen. The bad behavior of tiny people is bad behavior. The party line is that they will outgrow those things and because we have a merciful God, that's sometimes true. But deferring to others, taking turns and treating others the way we want to be treated are life lessons. They don't go away. These are the things we need to teach our children, starting when they are small. And we can never let up on the lesson plan until they are grown and gone. Then – and only then—can we start looking for a house on Easy Street.

GPS Kids

If it were up to me, my kids would never be allowed to leave the house. That way, I'd always know exactly where they are. *(The basement)*. And I'd know exactly what they're doing. *(Fighting over Xbox)*. However, their Dad actually allows them out. He's a freethinker....and it's a real pain for me. Where are they? What time will they come back? Who are they with? I'm haunted by The Control Freak Within.

That's why I've been thinking. The perfect solution would be to implant them with a microchip at the hospital. When? Why, the day they are born. I propose they'd be injected with a tiny GPS chip while still recovering from the trauma of birth. C'mon, it can't be any more painful than circumcision! A Geek Squad technician would show up to shoot a microchip in Junior's itty bitty foot or perhaps Sissy's teeny, tiny butt. Immunization records would show MMR and GPS. Perfect.

You know what a GPS is, right? A Global Positioning System. It's generally used to help clueless drivers find their way out of their neighborhood. I propose we use this great technology on our kids in case they leave the neighborhood. I call my invention GPS Kids.

Now, while the tots are little, Mom won't need to turn on the tracking device very often. For the first few years, those little critters fuss if Mom so much as closes the bathroom door. They keep us in sight 24/7. Even while we're playing peek-a-boo, they only cover half their face to keep us in sight.

No, it's only as they gain independence that we need this nefarious tool. For my kids, this was at about age eighteen...months. Once I almost called the police to report a missing toddler. I only hesitated because I could see that every door was still heavily locked; no one could get in or out. A GPS would have revealed that toddler Trevor had climbed into a kitchen cupboard and was taking a nap amongst my Pampered Chef. Yes, a GPS would have been handy that day.

Admit it; it's genius. No other technology is as clever or obsessive as GPS Kids. It's true that some cell phones do have tracking chips. This only allows parents to track the phone! Monica knows full well to leave her cell phone at the library while she's really at a concert being gleefully tossed into a Mosh Pit! Her uninformed mother, thrilled that Monica is diligently working on her term paper on Saturday night, mistakenly rolls over and sleeps in peace. In reality, only the cheap flip phone is safe and sound.

No, Concerned Parents, this is simply not enough. Let's band together, but we'll need to keep this a secret. No teen can know where we're getting our information. (Most of them would hack the chip out of their derrieres by dinner.) We need them to actually believe that we have eyes in the back of our heads. With GPS Kids, when they claim they were at the library and weren't, parents can yell, "You're grounded! You were in a Mosh Pit!" Ahh, the power!

Where does this Control Freak-ism come from? My selfish desire to relax. I can only truly relax when my five kids are safely in our home (and preferably in bed.) Unfortunately, my husband Dave waxes poetic about the grand adventures he and his brother had as kids. They never stayed home! Instead, they jumped off trains, swam through sewers, climbed up radio towers, and were home in time for dinner. Their mother never knew a thing and thus, never had a moment of concern.

Therefore, Dave thinks our teen boys should be getting into similar trouble. He'd like it if they had some shocking stories to tell us at family reunions in twenty years time. To get some adventure started, one summer he challenged our fourteen-year-old sons to ride to the mall. Imagine my chagrin. I don't even want them out of my sight. And their dad lets them cross the highway! On bikes. Without helmets!

Several friends called to tattle. "I saw your boys. Were they riding *to the mall?*" Shock, horror and disdain vibrated the telephone lines. "Their dad let them do it," I replied. Utter silence. Who can contradict a freewheelin', post-hippie dad? The battle is lost. Clearly, I need GPS Kids. That way, when my kids fall off a bike while traversing the interstate, I'll be the first to know. I'll be watching them on closed-circuit TV like some sick version of *The Truman Show*. It'll be great.

Final point. When would this chip be removed? I think right before their wedding night seems appropriate. Unless their wives decide to take over the monitoring. Hey, I'm just trying to help them out.

Shopping Spree

Lately all of the kids need new clothes. They have this pesky habit of growing every year. You'd think I would be used to it by now. They've been growing on and off since birth. But still, when they need new stuff, I always freak out. "Didn't we just get you those skateboarding shoes?" I cry out, visions of $65 dancing through my head. "Yeah, last fall," a boy will concur. I live in a fantasy world where each child only needs one new pair of shoes a year. Come to think of it, that's not fantasy, that's how I grew up. We always got new school shoes in August, before school began. Then we were stuck with 'em for the whole year. I never remember getting new shoes in the spring. Recently Danny had his entire foot sticking out from a huge hole in his shoes. It was May so I naturally suggested he duct tape them until school was out, then wear his flip flops until summer is over. For some reason, he was not hip to my plan. Nope, they need clothes and shoes. It's so annoying.

So lately, we've been doing a lot of shopping. It's best to take the teens out one at a time. It heads off the inevitable and annoying comparisons of what brother or sister is getting. Shopping is bad enough but the pouting can send me over the edge. And I pout very easily. Disagreements generally are part of a shopping trip and I don't care to have many witnesses to that scene.

A few years ago one of our sons was going through a stage that involved him coloring all of his fingernails black with Sharpie marker. (We wouldn't buy him black nail polish.) This was long before Adam Lambert of *American Idol* fame made that look commonplace. The black Sharpie nails were complimented with black t-shirts and skin tight jeans. Having recently been a teen myself, I knew it was just a stage so I played along. I also looked like an idiot in high school when I wore men's boxer shorts as outerwear, so I'm willing to cut my kids some slack. We trotted to one of the fierce stores at the mall to buy a pair of what my dear old dad called dungarees. You know, jeans?

At the mall, Danny was trying on these skin tight jeans. I was shocked he got into them without Crisco or going on that lemonade and hot pepper diet. He walked out, stiffly, as he couldn't bend at any point. I immediately challenged him to sit down or at least prove that he could breathe. I also wondered aloud if these pants would prohibit his ability to father a child one day. Our helpful salesperson showed up at just that moment to tell him how sexy and fantastic he looked in the jeans. (He was sold at sexy, believe me.) When I protested saying, "He can't walk, sit or breathe!" she took the time to explain to me that this is the style and if he's got it, flaunt it and a bunch of other nonsense from someone who clearly works on commission. He got the $60 jeans, wore them twice, ate lunch for a few days and outgrew them. He sold them to an emaciated friend for $15. What a deal.

The lesson I learned was this, "Let the kids have a say but when it's your money, you cast the deciding vote." I hope that you clip that sentence out and put it in your wallet for when you are at the mall with your own teenagers. If they want to buy weird, oddly fitted and horrific clothes in an attempt at self-expression, that's fine, they can pay for it themselves. I want to buy them things I'm not embarrassed about.

Back to our recent shopping trip(s). We were so thrilled to find a resale store with all teen clothes. I was actually there four different times in one week as my kids suddenly discovered that shorts are cool and needed them immediately. I have (almost) kept my mouth shut as they've worn jeans constantly over the last few summers, even when it was 103 degrees. They would say, "We're not hot." But now all of a sudden, they are hot and want shorts. This is the moment I've been waiting for. Shorts are back in! And they are the preppy plaid ones from when I was in college. The tag on one pair of shorts actually called them "Old School." Yup, that pretty much sums me up. In any case, full of secret glee, Old School got out her VISA and started chargin' it up. Finally, they are wearing clothes that I like! Just don't tell them I said so.

Dear Santa

Last year, next to the cookies and milk we left out for Santa, we found this note from our youngest child. It's a little window into our wacky world.

> Santa!
>
> Merry Christmas! Thank you for the presents! Please don't eat cookies in the living room or in the tree room. Or mom will get mad.
>
> Love, Julia
>
> P.S. Don't drink the milk in those rooms either…you don't want to spill. Please eat in the kitchen.

I was stunned. First of all, I didn't know that I was so rigid regarding the milk and cookies. Second of all, I didn't realize that we could cast all of our cares on Santa. I think Julia is onto something. Clearly she had worries that Santa would have an awful run-in with her mean mother. This year, I also have a lot on my mind. My biggest concern is actually not that St. Nick will smash a candy cane cookie on my beige carpet. So, following Julia's lead, I'm writing my own missive to the jolly old elf.

Dear Santa,

Thank you so much for taking care of all the gifts for Christmas. That is a big load off my mind. You see, I find life to be pretty complicated. It's good to know as this season approaches that you've got all the presents chosen and will deliver no extra charge. You are better than Amazon.com. Plus you don't charge a penny for these services. That's great because that's just about how much we have to invest in this holiday celebration.

There's a lot on my mind these days. You can't even believe how complicated life is outside of the North Pole. Santa, you don't seem like the worrying type. I bet you just sit back and let Mrs. Claus bring you a cup of warm milk at bedtime, then drift off to sleep. At our house, I'm Mrs. Claus. Nothing is easy, not even a glass of milk. You see, there are seven people living in my house and we buy four different types of milk. Skim, 1%, 2% and lactose free. (We cut out the chocolate soy in an effort to simplify our lives.) Enjoy your glass of milk, Santa.

Now Santa, please understand. You might think because of the four types of milk that I live with people who are difficult to please. Santa, that's not true. They are very easily pleased, as long as they get what they want.

> Alex would really like a Wii game system.
>
> Trevor would like permission to text.
>
> Danny would like his learners permit.
>
> Caroline would like to be a vet.
>
> Julia would like Webkins....again.
>
> Dave would like gas prices to stay in the $2 range.
>
> (And to somehow be teleported to a life of ease, post putting five kids through college. A house on a lake, perhaps, or with a mountain view? Or both. A simple cottage where he can eat cookies in every room.)
>
> Martie would like peace and love. And a self-cleaning house.

Santa, you rock! Since you've got these gifts covered, can I ask for just one more teeny weeny favor? Would it be possible, Santa, for you to cover holiday baking as well? We need cookies to go with all that milk. I used to make seven kinds from scratch. Back in the day, I began baking right after Thanksgiving in order to freeze tins full of holiday delights. (There are a lot of things I used to do. Sigh.) Now my holiday baking has been reduced to Fly-By Baking. I buy buckets of chocolate chip cookie dough and pass them off as homemade. (Oh, that's right; you already know that, don't you, Santa?) I would really like to have a lovely variety of homemade cookies. Can Mrs. Claus get involved in the outsourcing of that project?

Just tell her these few requirements. I've been watching my fat and it wobbles like your own bowl full of jelly. So some lower calorie cookies would be nice. We have dear friends with peanut allergies, so scratch the peanuts. I like walnuts, but Dave only eats pecans, so stick with those. And we love cookies, but not on the carpet. That's about it.

Phew, I feel my stress level reducing as this letter draws to a close. Santa, you are truly magical. I read that 75% of doctors visits are due to stress-related ailments. Headaches, insomnia, stomachaches. Check, check, check…been there, done that. So Santa, you are doing me a Big, Fat, Elfin-Magic-Sized Favor to take care of all these worries. My head feels lighter, I think I can sleep tonight, and my belly is neither tense nor rumbly. I feel the holiday spirit just expanding in me (where the cookie dough used to sit). No gifts to buy, no bills to pay, no cookies to bake. This will indeed be a Merry Christmas.

So get to work, Big Guy. And help yourself to cookies and milk…in the kitchen of course.

Your #1 fan,
Martie

PS. I drink the skim.

Last One on the Bus

My youngest child was heading off to kindergarten. You can't imagine my excitement. I had five kids in six years and had survived four long-distance moves. I was anticipating a little "me" time and it was about five years overdue. I was not going to cry. I was going to go out to brunch and get a manicure. That was my plan.

The four eldest children skipped off to the bus stop without a backwards glance. When I called and cried to the school district, they gave us our own bus stop at the bottom of the driveway. All I needed to do was wave from the front porch. The big kids skipped away and hopped on board. They were probably relieved to get out from under my mood swings and insane insistence that they both wipe and flush.

Little Julia seemed excited about her chance to join the big kid team by going to school. Again, not as excited as I was, but pretty dang excited. We had pumped her up with incredible stories about pencil boxes, little cartons of milk and story time. She knew most of her ABCs although she got fuzzy around "l-m-n-o-p." She sang, "Elmo Elmo P" and since she was the baby of the family, we just laughed and cautioned each other to never correct her. It was just so darn cute. Yes, she was ready.

Here was my Back to School plan. I would take six to eight weeks recovering from having had tiny people underfoot for the last seven years. Then, I was going to scrub the house from top to bottom with all the spare time I had. Next, I would paint all the walls and then I would have time to teach Bible study and bring meals to shut-ins. I had a plan.

Our elementary school is just two miles up the road. All five Byrd kids would be at the same school for one famous year. They'd get on and off the bus together, leaving me alone from

7:04 a.m. until 2:21 p.m. Ah, the bliss. The first day of school dawned bright and hot. I stayed in my pj's to wave goodbye from the front porch. Alex, Daniel, Trevor and Caroline all boarded the bus. Julia stalled out.

She started to cry. Then wail. I ran down the driveway in my mismatched pajamas. She attached herself to my leg and wouldn't let go. I tried to pry her loose and put her on the first step of the bus. That didn't fly as she screamed in terror. Our long-suffering bus driver raised her eyebrows at me. I conceded, "Go on ahead" and shouted to the other kids, "It's okay!" So much for my relaxing morning. So much for staying in my pajamas.

"What happened?" I asked Julia when she had calmed down. She replied, "The first step was just so big."

Oh honey girl, you are right. You are so, so right. The first step is so big. It always is. It's the hardest one to get on. But you can't go anywhere without making that leap.

I threw on some clothes and brought my little one to school that day. Her kindergarten teacher, Mrs. Forbes, introduced her to a little girl named Jenna and explained that they would ride the bus home together. (They went on to share a seat –and all their secrets and birthdays and joys-- for the next six years.) As I left her in the classroom, something surprising happened. I started to cry.

The first step is just so big for moms, too.

Honor Your Mother…or Else

Nothing like having a few teenagers to take the wind out of your sails. My little lovelies, for instance, take near constant delight in correcting me. It's hard to imagine that I've misspoken, mispronounced or misjudged as often as I do now that I have a houseful of teens. They constantly point out my errors. It's like living in a minefield.

"That's not how you say it, Mom!"
"You just told us that a second ago!"
"I told you that first. Geez!"

Humble, her name is Mother of Teens. Mother of Teens is not paid in butterfly kisses and dandelion bouquets like her sister, Mother of Toddlers. Oh no, those days are long gone. Yet there are so many benefits to having Big Kids, as I lovingly call my teens. As a Mother of Teens, I extract my payment, er, <u>love</u> in other ways.

Consider this. Big kids can carry in all the groceries…and put them all away. Big kids can wash the car…and drive it to the library to return my overdue library books. They can cut their own toenails, brush their own teeth and in general, do all their own personal hygiene. (When they feel like it, that is.) Big Kids can make dinner …and do the dishes afterwards. It's a delight. When you have teens, every day is Mother's Day.

Now some might say that Mother's Day is just another Hallmark holiday. Cynics. Many mothers would protest coyly, "I don't need a whole entire day!" while secretly wondering why a three-day weekend wouldn't be more commemorative. I think that Hallmark took over where preschool teachers left off. Think about it. Preschool teachers do a glorious job with their Mother's Day celebrations. I once was so desperate for recognition, I bought a new van so I wouldn't miss the

Mother's Day Tea at preschool. That artwork with our child's handprint still occupies a position of honor in the kitchen. Once out of preschool, however, the Love Fest Ends. It's each child for himself. That's why we need Hallmark to remind, guilt or otherwise plague our offspring into sheepishly recognizing us, if only once a year.

Moms, relax. The accolades will come. They might not come on Mother's Day. They may not be in a card that cost $4.95 and plays "Wild Thing." But you'll feel the love, in various ways, as your Big Kids become adults. Here are some moments I've either experienced or dreamed about:

Academic Award Day. You've stopped paying attention because the child being lauded sounds so perfect, so gifted, and so wonderful that you know it can't be yours. As you're digging in your purse for a stick of gum, you hear your own child's name called! With tears of pride, you realize your tissues are in the car...with the camera.

High School Field Trip Day. Other people's sons and daughters fight to be in your car because they heard you are cool and that you stock in Skittles for the ride as well as let them listen to their radio station full blast. Your child can't suppress a grin because, hey, that's my mom.

Poker Day. You cajole your way into the game with a bunch of hairy teens who laugh at you and your ineptitude...until you win every hand.

Graduation Day. In the commencement address your valedictorian quotes Abraham Lincoln: *"Everything I am or ever hope to be, I owe to my angel mother."*

Wedding Day. The bride-to-be sobs in gratitude as she thanks you for raising the perfect mate for her. In particular she is grateful that he always lifts the seat and takes out the trash without being asked.

First Grandchild. They've decided to honor their sweet mother by naming their baby girl after you.

Okay, burst the fantasy bubble, Mom! This last one is where my kids draw the line. I've floated these dreams out there and no one is cooperating. Julia did name her obese Lots-To-Love doll Baby Martie in hopes of satisfying me. I was oddly pleased. I'll take what I can get!

So hang on, Mothers of Teens. Hang on, even if you have to make your own breakfast on Mother's Day. Hang on, even as you make dinner reservations so you don't have to cook on your special day. You are loved. Dearly loved. The teens just like to keep it a secret, is all. But your day is coming. They'll honor their mother one day. I've seen it in my dreams.

Wake Up and Smell the Coffee

Getting seven people up and out of the house in less than an hour is a ton of fun. I have pitched this concept to the networks as the latest reality show. It would be called *Wake Up and Smell the Coffee*. It would be a family competition and I know the Byrds could win big bucks. We could use the cash.

Dad would be team captain. He actually wakes up every morning without an alarm clock. You might say he wakes up with the birds (the other ones.) He works out at 5 o'clock in the morning. By 6:30 a.m., he's been up for hours and is ready for some company. He cheerfully wakes up all the kids. Cheerful is an understatement. He actually channels the Robin William's character in *Good Morning, Vietnam*. He wakes them up with songs, comedy numbers and character sketches. He lets me sleep. (I'm not a Robin Williams fan.)

Caroline, Julia, Daniel and Trevor are all woken up in the 6 o'clock hour. As you can imagine, there is a mad rush for the shower and lots of door pounding, accented with "Hurry up!" and "I left my toothbrush in there!" or the forlorn cry, "Can someone bring me a towel?"

At seventeen, Alex has a very hard time waking up. He comes alive after midnight so morning is just not his thing. He sets his cell phone as an alarm. It goes off at 6:30 and every 5 minutes thereafter. As a backup, he sets the alarm on his iHome, the iPod deck. That alarm goes off every 10 minutes. Alarm bells are ringing at 6:30, 6:35, 6:37, 6:40, 6:45, 6:47...you get the drill. Seems like it should wake even the most fatigued teen but no. Alex refuses to get up. He stays in bed until someone yells, "Alex! It's 7 o'clock!" Then he springs into action.

Alex is a tenacious competitor. He can shower, dress, eat breakfast, brush his teeth, and corral his siblings into the car in twenty-five minutes or less. Alex would be an awesome contestant in the *Wake Up* Reality Show. Everyone would want to be on his team. Plus he wouldn't slow anyone down with silly things like pleasant conversation. He's fast and silent.

His alarms really bother his loving mother. Why? Because I'm still enjoying my sleep and I don't like to hear the jarring bells and odd song selections. Julia says his alarm sounds like the scary monkey music in *The Wizard of Oz*. Clearly, this is upsetting, even all the way down the hall. Yet he is immune. When complaining about it the other morning, the whole family chimed in on how irritating his alarms are to us. Dad said, "What alarms? I never hear a thing." Dad is relentlessly upbeat in the morning. I am not. Therefore, I opt to stay in bed as long as possible.

My goal is to stay in bed until three things happen. One, I hear the coffee grinding. Two, I smell it brewing. Three, I hear the bus pass by. Then and only then do I emerge from my room. Julia is our only child who still rides the school bus. It comes at 7:04 every morning. Hearing the bus pass is Julia's signal to get her coat on. It's also my signal to hop out of bed. Julia wants a "Mommy and Daddy sandwich" before she leaves in the morning. This is when you hug with your child stuck in the middle. I have just enough time to enjoy sandwiching JB before she gets on the bus.

Speaking of sandwiches, they are a big part of the morning routine. Happy Daddy (one of Dave's comedy characters) runs a sandwich shop in our kitchen. He keeps up a hilarious patter of jokes as he makes peanut butter and jelly sandwiches. Because special orders don't upset Happy Daddy, the kids expect to have it their way. Some like crunchy. Some like creamy. Some like their sandwich loaded with peanut butter. Others like extra jelly.

Mom likes coffee. And I like to stay out of the sandwich

business whenever humanly possible. I'm so thankful for Happy Daddy. (When Happy Daddy goes out of town on business, Crabby Mommy instructs the kids to buy lunch at school.)

It may sound like Grand Central station, but I'm telling you, we've got it down! Part of our routine is someone forgetting something important. The kids have a habit of singling out the item that is most critically important to a successful day. They put these items on the kitchen island while muttering, "This way I won't forget it."

For decades, I have been saying, "Put it in your backpacks!" Or the variations, "Did you put it in your folder? Did you put it in your gym bag? Did you put it in your binder?" But no, these kids know better. Their system is to put the most important item on the island. It may be the paper they typed until the wee hours. It may be their uniform for the big game. It may be the recorder they absolutely must have for music class today. It may be a library book that has to be turned in or else. It is super, really, very important stuff.

Naturally, they proceed to the car laden with bags, lunches, and backpacks. It's crazy how much they have to carry to school each day. Sadly, routinely, daily, they forget the island items. This is when I spring into action. In my bare feet, gigantic red bathrobe and bed head, I sprint after them, flailing the forgotten item. This must amuse the neighbors. I know it will be the funniest part of the *Wake Up and Smell the Coffee* reality show. I'd howl with laughter seeing a crazy mom running after the bus with a SpongeBob lunch box and a recorder. As long as it's not me, that is.

I'm starting to wonder if they do it on purpose. Running after them is how Crabby Mommy shows her love.

We've Got Short Shorts

A famous Nair commercial from the seventies boasted, "Nair for short shorts." This was an advertisement, not a warning. Looking back, that ad should have made us run and hide. See, the fashion required we slather ourselves in toxic waste to remove every speck of hair so we could pull on miniscule outerwear with confidence. That was then and apparently, this is now. Yes, it's back again. The dreaded short short. But now it's worse. Now I'm a mom.

On a recent shopping trip with the kids I was thrilled to see that the boys chose big, preppy, plaid shorts that were popular in the eighties when I was in college. They are so long and wide that if a girl was wearing them, they would be called gauchos. They are fully covered, these boys, and although their legs are quite hairy, they are blessedly covered by madras plaid and we can all sleep in peace.

But the girls, oy vay, what they are wearing these days. I was horrified when I saw the short shorts that my middle school girls are interested in. All the girls at the store were wearing them and it's obvious to me that these shorts are no larger than the average Splenda packet. When I called them Splenda shorts, my girls harrumphed and stormed away mad. I think I'm being hilarious but they are not laughing. I am laughing but it's in a slightly hysterical manner, come to think of it.

Discussing it with a dear friend, she agreed with my Splenda packet assessment. She shared that her daughter's friend has such short shorts that when she wears them, and I quote, "her baby maker was showing." Having once been inadvertently but traumatically flashed by a male camp counselor during the era when OP short shorts were in for both men and women, I knew exactly what she was describing and it's not pretty.

Stop the madness, Splenda Short Wearers! Every mother I know wants to wrap you up in a beach towel and smuggle you out of gym class. I blame Beyonce even though I don't know if she's ever worn those shorts. I blame her for making booty cool. And Jennifer Lopez, you too. How would you feel if your little baby twins wanted to wear those tiny clothes when they are in high school and hormones are running amuck without any help from skimpy clothes? What would Jenny from the Hood say then?

Cover the booty and the boobies, too, girls. Leave a little something to the imagination. If the gown you wear for a physical is ten times the fabric of what you wear to school, you know there's something wrong. I'm not saying we should go back to bustles and gowns but can we at least cover a little skin? As the mother of three boys, I'm begging you.

Freaky Twilight Moms

Since the dawn of *Harry Potter*, I've made it a policy to read what my kids are reading. I do this cheerfully as I love to read and it's a fun way to have at least one thing in common with my teens. Do I read everything? Nah. For instance, recently they got into a very long series of animated Japanese-style comic books. I checked out, literally, after flipping through the first book. What's to discuss? I can imagine myself starting with: "Did you like the sketch of the guy karate-chopping the other guy?" "Mom, get a life." However, the anime books kept even my non-readers reading and we requested about eighty-nine inter-library loans in order to see every last tae kwon do move.

Literature heavy on hobbits or dragons don't get my blood pumping, but other than that, I really enjoy peering into their taste in what we used to call literature. When they were younger, I would bribe them to read with the offer of a private Book Club with me. If they read *Old Yeller* or *Little House on the Prairie*, I'd take them out to dinner and discuss the book. After a while, that idea became "lame." I ratcheted up to pure bribes. After enjoying *The Shack*, I offered each of my kids $5 if they would read and discuss it. Only Caroline took me up on my offer and sadly only got $3 into the story before she was lured back to a series with cats as the protagonists.

To really discuss books with teens, you have to read what they're reading. And just FYI, Harry Potter is so Last Year. The hip kids are reading the *Twilight* series by Stephenie Meyer. (And if they say they're not, they're lying.) Everyone has read at least one in this popular (42 million sold!) series. These books even caused my son Daniel to ask, "Do you think books can be addictive?" (Posed after a cumulative sixteen reads, he has good reason to be concerned!)

With that kind of question, I was more compelled than ever to hop on the bandwagon and see what all the fuss was about.

Hearing only that it was a genre called Vampire Romance, I picked up the first book gingerly, as if it would bite me. I thought I was the only person over fourteen who was reading the books. Turns out I'm not alone. Although initially written for an adolescent audience, this series is popular from middle school through menopause. (Warning for parents: the romance heats up as the books progress. The first two books are pretty PG but by the final consummation, yikes, it's getting pretty close to a R.)

What's it all about? Dreamy, hunkish vampire love for a girl who just simply can't believe she's anything special. Everyone who reads *Twilight* is transported back to high school when we also suspected we weren't special but swooned if we were noticed by the football captain, not the Living Dead. After only a few pages, I could see why Danny asked the question. The books actually did suck the life out of me as I devoted every waking hour to completing the series of four books over three hypnotic days last summer.

As a lark, my Book Club decided to read Twilight. We are a proper group of ladies who generally dip into *The Good Earth* or *The Secret Life of Bees*. We have a little wine and cheese and are both jovial and erudite. The Twilight Book Club was being held at my home. After one member offered to bring virgin Bloody Marys, I knew we were in for a serious theme night. I put on a blood red shirt, baked a cake with a vampire face, and invited Danny to be our guest speaker. The Book Club was getting hip!

To add some panache to the discussion, I got online and was flummoxed to find over twelve thousand variations of Twilight themed t-shirts. Good news! All come in adult sizes. I laughed at my favorite t-shirt line for at least two weeks. See, the stories are set in a town called Forks, Washington. The best t-shirt sported the line, "Meanwhile, in a town called Spoons." I wanted it, size medium. Does that make me a Twilight Mom?

Freaky Twilight Mom is more like it! I am only going to wear my Twilight themed t-shirt around the house…or possibly when we go to Williamsburg this summer. Surprisingly, my teens were really into it. I asked, "Do you think it's weird that Mom read *Twilight* for book club?" and they said, "Nah, it's cool!"

Danny did a dynamite job as our guest speaker at book club and explained how he relates more to the Werewolf than the Vampire. It all but garnered applause. Do you read this as an endorsement for the monsters-among-us books? That's not my point. My point is this. I endorse reading! And I'm willing to go where my kids lead. I read *The Naked Olympics* prior to a book report on Ancient Greek competitions; it had scary illustrations. Reading their books has made for some lively dinner conversations. Think about it. Why discuss who is next to go on the Reality TV Show Du Jour? How about we talk about books?

It's so crazy, it works. Read along with your teens. Tell 'em Freaky Twilight Mom sent you.

Because I Said So

Many of us grew up in the era of Sesame Street, Dr. Spock, and the *Free to be...You and Me* tape from Marlo Thomas and friends. Even in the most conventional families, the 70's insisted that parents who didn't know the answer wouldn't just blunder their way through. Instead, they'd say, "Let's look that up together, sweetheart" while pulling out the A-D Volume from the family's hardbound set of Encyclopedia Britannica.

This created a faulty understanding that kids and parents were somehow equals and would muddle through life together. The result? Confused Gen X'ers who don't know how to raise kids. They don't know who is boss, them or the kids. They seem to think family life is a democracy. What a joke. Figuring it out together might work with little kids but when you have teens, forget it. It's war. Parents, if you let them know how much you don't know, you've lost. You've lost the battle and you've lost the war.

Face it, parents. Teens these days have a lot more than a dog-eared encyclopedia on their side. These kids have the whole world in their hands. There's one word that has forever changed the face of parenting: Internet.

No longer will the beloved words "Because I say so" carry the weight they did back in the day. Now teens with Blackberries finger their keyboard and announce, "But Mom! 75% of parents allow their kids to drive before they actually have a license." Peer pressure has gone global. No longer am I challenged by the standards of the neighborhood. Now I have to know that kids in France drink wine with dinner. I always said "knowledge is power" until my kids got Internet access. Then I changed my catchphrase to "knowledge is annoying." And Mommy is right, repeat after me, Mommy is right, right, right!

"If your friends all jumped off a bridge, would you jump?" That used to be a parental power statement designed to stop unthinking teens in their tracks. Now it's viewed as an idiotic non-sequitur. "Of course I'd jump, Mom, I watch *Extreme Sports* all the time and no one ever gets hurt!" The "DUH!" is implied.

Oh. Right. You saw it on YouTube. That kid lived. Clearly you are right, son, and I am wrong. What happened to *Father Knows Best*? (The philosophy as well as the TV show.) I loved programs which portrayed dads as all-knowing. Ward Cleaver never said, "Gee, Beaver, I don't know, why don't you Google it?" Dads, act like you know; fake it 'til you make it. As we say about our own beloved dad, "Not always right, but never in doubt." Right or wrong, he's not backing down. Way to go, Honey!

When I was little, there was actually a show whose title was *Wait 'til your Father Gets Home*. The implication? You're gonna get it! Your dad will set you straight, young man. Now every program on TV could be titled *Teens Run the Planet* and subtitled *Parents are Stupid Idiots*. If parents are characters at all, they only drop by to ruin the teens good time. This is cable TV at its finest.

This rampant disrespect bugs me. Some shows don't even try to hide their disdain in the titles! Think of this one....*Fairly Odd Parents*. Why I never! Fairly Odd Parents?! So what, we all are. That doesn't mean you shouldn't listen to us! Then there was Nickelodeon's *Zoey 101*. It starred teen role-model Jamie Lynn Spears. You could tune in and see that her parents didn't slow her down one bit. She's living away from home at fifteen. She wears skimpy tops and never attends class at her cushy prep school. It's a pretend-college with million dollar décor. The parents simply foot the bill and clearly, that's all they're good for. The program was marketed to tweens until, darn it, Jamie Lynn got pregnant and the show was cancelled. What a shame.

I'm hard-core. I won't even let my kids watch *The Simpsons* because Bart speaks disrespectfully to his parents. However, Bart seems like Bobby Brady compared to the kids on TV today. I'm ready to bring back the old adage about children being seen and not heard. Am I the only one?

Elise and Eileen are college friends of mine who have school-aged kids. They are already exhausted from the parental rhetoric. Real-life conversations almost sent them over the bleeding edge. If all the other kids jumped off a bridge, would you? Oh, you would? Well, I wouldn't let you. So there.

Since it is war and all, my friends thought of a clever retaliation. They make hip t-shirts where the joke is on the kids. Their company is called Planet Mom. I want to move to that planet. I get on www.planetmomtshirts.com just to pick up some snappy responses to use with the kids.

I bought a few of their shirts. I wear the **Secretary of Transportation** one every time I drive on a field trip. But my favorite t-shirt actually asserts **Because I Said So**. That's my line! I simply loved it. Every parent who saw it also loved it. The shirt said it all. I wore it nearly every day until it mysteriously disappeared in the wash. That's the last time my children do my laundry. That wasn't just a shirt; it was my suit of armor.

Should I Get Bangs?

Women are concerned with the darndest things. First, our weight. I recently lost twenty-something pounds. Now I say twenty-something so you might think it was twenty-nine lbs, when really it was twenty-one lbs. Why say twenty-something? I want to impress you. Why? Because I'm a woman and we want to impress each other. We want to impress each other, look like each other and agree with each other. Women ask each other's opinion on the oddest things.

Like recently, I was on the Weight Watcher discussion boards, online. It's where you can ask each other the best way to choke down steel cut oats in the morning and how to sneak extra vegetable servings into your…well, everything. Occasionally women post things akin to family secrets. Stuff like, "I want to murder my sister- in-law because she is clearly trying to sabotage my weight loss by bringing mac 'n cheese to our family reunion." Anyway, these are several hundred thousand of my closest friends.

This summer I was wrestling with a big issue, as women do, and so I decided to post my big question online on the WeightWatchers website, to ask my new best friends. Here was my question:

"Should I get bangs?"

Thirty-five women wrote back. Not one has ever met or seen me. That's just how women are. We care.

At least I think we care. I have four sisters. We care. I was so touched a few years back when I saw my twin sister after an absence of a year. "When did you get that?" she asked immediately, pointing to a new freckle on my neck. Not even my dermatologist would notice such a thing, but my sister did. She noticed. She asked. She cared.

I have been obsessed with my hair for years. There, I said it. This is because I have had a very long history of bad haircuts. And it's not that I haven't thrown thousands of dollars at the problem because I have. I was in my mid-thirties before I learned that most women color their hair. Every woman I know does except for Claire and her hair is perfect and it's just God's gift to her.

I've had bangs since I was a baby so you wouldn't imagine it would be the burning question that I would post online for discussion. I have an increasingly wrinkled forehead so again, what's the mystery? Clearly keep that covered with hair. But I don't want to miss a good trend and besides, I can't stand to have hair in my face. The bang trend seems to call for the long, side swept bangs. I can't stand to have even a strand of hair over my left eye as the style demands. And history has shown that I am not current with my hairstyle so why start now, in the middle of my life?

Should I get bangs? The discussion board was nearly unanimous in their assent. All they had to go on was my starting and current weight and my screen name by which they deduced my age. (I put my birth year in my screen name…silly, I know.) Armed with only my weight and age, they all said yes, get bangs. Wanting to please my new friends and also show that I'm not one of those women who ask for advice and then never take it, I ran right out and got bangs.

I asked for short bangs, though, or as I described them "third grade bangs." Bucking the trends is my signature look, I guess.

No Excuses

My mantra this year is "No Excuses." Are Christians allowed to have mantras? No matter….call it a breath prayer, a focus, a Divine Order from the Holy Spirit. This is going to be the Year of No Excuses.

It's going to be tough. It's in our very nature to make excuses. From the very first days of the very first humans, excuses and finger-pointing were the order of the day. Consider this. Satan, in the form of the snake, blames God. "Did He really tell you that? He doesn't want you to have what He has," he says to Eve. Our sister Eve, after making a bad choice, blames the snake, "That snake told me to eat it…." Then Adam *(Oh, this is bad)* blames *both* Eve *and* God. "That woman *You gave me* made me eat it" he excuses himself to his Creator God. Oh brother!

See, excuse-making is deeply engrained. Our precious children make excuses for their bad behavior. Sometimes they even blame me. "My mother told me to do it." I was complaining about this character trait to my friend Amy the Psychologist. I was excusing them as being sinful little ones who were born this way. She gently said, "Yes, it's ingrained in us…but children usually imitate what they see most." Busted! She was kindly, lovingly saying to me, "They got it from you, sister." And you know what? They did.

I have a hard time standing my ground. It's hard to decide what I should do and what I should avoid doing. Like the Biblical woman Martha, I rush around doing it all and then complain to the Lord, "Why isn't anyone helping me?" But the Lord didn't tell me to do it all. That's my own nature ensnaring me. I say yes when I mean no, and then I use excuses to dig myself out of the pit I've made.

There's a great verse that says "Let your yes be yes and your no be no." Sounds reasonable, right? But am I the *only one* who says "yes" when I know I should say "no"? Yes is simply easier to say. Yes, I'll bring cookies. Yes, I'll work the Book Fair. Yes, I'll teach Sunday School, bring a meal, watch your kids. After about fifty yeses, though, we collapse under the impossibility of being All-Things-to-All-People and we realize that some of those yeses are going to have to be nos.

Get this! I have been so ensnared over the years in my insane yes-saying that I have actually rejoiced in a strep throat diagnosis, or a barfing kid, or a dead car battery, as seemingly legitimate ways to get out of the over-commitments I have made. After all, those things are "not my fault." I gloried in being prescribed bed rest during my twin pregnancy. That was an awesome excuse to not proofread the new church directory. That's not normal, is it?

Many of us are positively great at excuses. We want to give an explanation that leaves us smelling like a rose. We make an excuse that says "I would have but....." What we're actually saying is, "Hey, it's not my fault!" I know I said I would but…I have a sick kid at home, I just found out I'm pregnant, it's raining out, my husband is running late. But, but, but….On and on it goes. There's got to be a better way. Here's an idea. How about being woman enough to say no in the first place?

Sometimes we know in our heart of hearts we will not be able to honor our commitments. Don't say yes and take it back later. Just say no! Then, if necessary, be grown-up enough to give the favor of an explanation, rather than an excuse, to the committee heads, neighbors and friends you are possibly disappointing. We can explain and be honorable. Whether they accept our no and our explanation is their issue, not ours.

Instead of blaming our kids or our life for our inability to serve, volunteer, show up or be a member, why don't we tell the truth? I'd love to hear someone say, "I only said "yes" so you would like me. You see, I was afraid you wouldn't like me if I said I couldn't be on your committee." Or "I have a strong need for affirmation so I said yes when you asked me to be Soccer Mom. The truth is I'm a terrible soccer mom."

By now, there are some PTA presidents who are steaming over this message. I know there are, because I've been the president of things before and it's positively aggravating how many people are good at saying no. That's not what I'm talking about. We do have projects to do. We do have places to go and people to see. We're not here on this earth for an extended vacation. That's true.

This is different. What I'm working on this year is learning how to pray for wisdom and direction *before* I make a single commitment. And when because of my fast speaking, low-esteeming, over-committing and under-praying personality, I've gotten in a jam, this will be the year of No Excuses. I will not make excuses or cast blame. Instead, I will be scrupulously honest in giving explanation of why I can't do what I said I would do. And I will say no. Without apology.

No excuses.

Darn you, Yahoo News!

I have just a few minutes to check some emails and possibly my bank balance. Yet You sit there, luring me with the news of the day. I can't help myself. My finger clicks the button. I just have to know, *"What are the fibs men tell on their first date?"* In the blink of an eye, my few precious moments of time are sucked down the time vacuum of the internet. And believe me, I'm none the wiser.

It might be a stretch to call it news, actually. Here are some of the teaser headlines I can't resist. Starbuck sales down 30%. Swine flu now in all fifty states. Investments you'd be an idiot to make. Five things you should never eat right before bedtime. How to lose ten pounds without even trying.

Can you tell which ones are the real headlines? Me, either. They are all so juicy and so easy to read. Does this constitute as news? Really? Because it's going down pretty easily, I'm not gonna lie. And I'm one of those dinosaurs who insisted that the Evening News would never disappear and that daily newspapers would be printed until Jesus comes back in glory.

Except I don't watch the Evening News. And I don't subscribe to the newspaper. I get my news from my husband, who is in his car a lot for work, and thus hears a lot of non-Yahoo-News. I also flip through *People* magazine at the dentist's office. Yup, my source for all information is Yahoo News. I'm getting basically the Juicy Fruit Gum version of news. And I'm okay with that.

My Real News aversion was a slight problem during the last election. Candidate research consisted of me voting on polls with questions like, *"Which candidate would you allow to watch your children?"* Yahoo news kept me so occupied with fluff that I didn't even know what the issues really were. I know who I voted for. The one I'd let babysit.

Hold that thought, I have to go check something. Okay, I'm back. I was lured for another look and had to follow the rabbit down the trail. Seems that yet another aged movie star has just impregnated a young co-star with his, and I quote, "love child." *Click to read comments from his wife and six other children!* For shame, for shame.

I'm scolding myself. I'm contributing to the madness by reading this stuff. It's my fault that there are paparazzi helicopters over private island weddings. I just want to catch a quick glimpse. I pride myself that I don't buy the magazines at the checkout lines. I don't let those rags into the house. But the internet is always on at home. And Yahoo News is my guilty pleasure. I can't turn away. Help!

Memory? What Memory?

The kids have been asking me to write this piece for a while, but frankly, it's slipped my mind. They are concerned about my memory. "What memory?" I retort. You see, I remember when my brain was like a steel trap. That I do remember. There was a time when I didn't have to write myself a note, set buzzers on my cell phone or ask other people to remind me of things. That was then, this is now. As my beloved Trevor recently noted, "I can remember when I was three years old and you can't remember two weeks ago." (Fooled him! I can't remember two hours ago!)

They say if you lose your memory, you still have it somewhere. (My theory is it is in with all the socks missing from the dryer as well as the kid's shot records, birth certificates, and the like.) If I still have it somewhere, I hope it will move back in when the kids move out. In case that doesn't happen, though, I'm keeping their scrapbooks up-to-date. Pictures actually jog our memory and in many cases, make the memory. Since I only take pictures of the happy moments (birthdays, proms, etc.), we'll all conclude in time that our life at home was one big party. The piles of laundry, temper tantrums and disgusting bathroom sinks will not be pictured and therefore, forever forgotten.

My teens are actually concerned about my wifty-ness. One suggested that I carry a notebook around to make note of things I want to remember. I explained that I tried that method, but was always forgetting the notebook. He told me to write in the notebook to remember the notebook. Hahaha, that is so funny I forgot to laugh! He either has a future in comedy or as an aide to senior citizens.

The faulty memory is not necessarily a family trait. For instance, my mother and sister don't put any names in their cell phones. They just memorize the numbers. They know everyone's number. They think it's <u>fun</u> to memorize numbers. I, on the other hand, don't remember numbers. Any numbers. If I lost my phone, I'd only be able to call my husband and, on a good day, 911.

My mind used to be very sharp. When I turned 35, I took what neurologists call a "cognitive step down." (Turns out it was an escalator to the bottom floor.) I started "compensatory skills" at that time…like writing things down. I write it all down on my calendar. If it's not on the calendar, it's not happening. (Except starting laundry, making coffee and unloading the dishwasher, I do those things on autopilot)

Everything else is on the calendar. Here's a typical day:

Work
Groceries
Julia off bus 2:20
Kids' Drama practice 3-5:30
Pick up kids!

This is how I manage. If I don't get it down, I don't get it done. No kidding, I have to write down "work" so I remember to go! Even things that repeat, every week, at the same time, for year after year after year, I write down. "Bible Study, Wednesdays, 10-12" got tedious to write so I printed out a label and slapped it on 52 weeks out of the year. Not noting it was not an option. It's the only way to ensure I'll be there.

I once read a story about Ronald Reagan. Apparently he kept a desk journal, like mine, and wrote down everything. As the story goes, one day mid- January, his Day-Timer read:

Get up
Shower

Read Bible

Eat Breakfast

Get inaugurated.

I can't actually recall where I saw that story, but I've repeated it a lot. I don't think I made it up, but who knows, I could have. The point being, very successful people need to jog their memories once in a while. Or once in an hour. But they are still beloved and don't necessarily all go on to develop Alzheimer's.

Why is my memory so swiss-cheesey? I have to give credit to the kids. Each one of them cost me hundreds of billions of brain cells during pregnancy. (This, again, is not scientifically verifiable, but ask other parents and they'll agree....kids make you dumb. Kids will also agree their parents are dumb, especially after age 13). I turned to my beloved Google to verify this for you. *"Some reasons for post pregnancy memory loss are lack of sleep, improper diet, birth, and lactation."* You ask me, the real cause of post pregnancy memory loss is KIDS.

Once I was leaving church after a lovely Mother's Morning Out. I spoke with my friend Jeanette in the parking lot for a while, but was bothered thinking I'd forgotten something. Oh yes! I forgot my Bible! I ran back into the church to grab the Bible and was accosted by the childcare worker. "We were wondering when you were coming to get your baby," she said knowingly. Oh right, I knew I forgot something important. Julia. (And she's a keeper.)

So, it's irritating to forget to pick up milk and bread. But in truth, there are some great benefits to the Loose Mom Memory. It causes the kids to be responsible for their own library books, school schedules and soccer cleats. After asking me seventy-five times, "Do you know where I left my _____?" the kids develop this odd habit of keeping track of their own stuff. (Mostly.) It's sheer delight. It's also fantastic to see how the kids are learning to write down their work schedules, start grocery lists and already begin to take care of me in my old age. They are definitely five things I will never forget.

Asked and Answered

I went through a period of time (okay, about five years) when I watched every *Law and Order* that came on TV. One summer I made it my goal to watch *Law and Order* at least once a day and I easily met and exceeded that goal. Yes, I could have been using that time to read the classics or learn counted cross stitch but I didn't. I watched *Law and Order*. I credit the show with one of my very favorite parenting lines of all time.

In the court, when a witness is being badgered by the prosecution, the defense attorney on *Law and Order* leaps up and says, "Asked and answered!" He holds up his hand like a traffic cop and glares angrily at the prosecuting attorney and imploringly at the judge. This one phrase snaps the judge to attention and he often tells the annoying prosecutor to move on or some such instruction. I love it.

When my children start to badger me like the prosecution, I have adopted this method. I hold up my hand and say, "Asked and answered." They just simply hate it. It goes something like this.

"Can I have a friend over?"

"No."

"Why? Why can't I? You said I could have a friend over later in the week? Why not today?"

"Asked and answered."

It's genius. Go ahead, try it. But here's my warning, moms and dads. You have to say it and walk away. Don't under any circumstance get sucked into defending your position after you've dropped the "asked and answered" bomb. You don't owe them an explanation. You are the parent and that's it.

It's the *Law and Order* version of "Because I said so." But it's ever so clever. It really works, even in reruns.

YahYah in the Jungle

Our oldest son, Alex, is the first to leave home. He left for the adventure of his lifetime. He is in Costa Rica on a Discipleship training program. He's with a great mission organization called Answering the Call. We love their ministry and the people. We trust them completely.

Alex worked hard to earn money for this trip. He mowed lawns, stood in as a line referee at soccer games and scrubbed floors at Chick-fil-A. He was also blessed by family and friends who contributed money and prayers to make his trip happen. Alex is in Costa Rica for the entire month of June. At seventeen, this is the farthest he's ever traveled. It's by far the longest time he's been away from home.

Mommy misses her YahYah.

When our twins were little, they couldn't pronounce "Alex." They called their heroic big brother YahYah. They outgrew the nickname but I still cling to it. There is a large part of my brain and heart in which little YahYah still lives. Just nineteen months older than Daniel and Trevor, he was always the leader. Beginning when he was three and they were two, his battle cry was, "C'mon, Bruvvers!" They would scramble to follow him climb a tree, pee outdoor or pile things up in order to crash them back down again. They never questioned his plans or if they would get in trouble. Alex was the boss or as I call him, the King of the Kids.

Alex has always been daring, brave and true. We have photographic evidence? Every year we take pictures of him doing back flips off a cement bridge at Lake Linganore. He flips into the lake at Uncle Dan's house every summer. I always insist Dan check the water depth on his sonar fish finder. Even so, I can't even watch. After he flips, he then sprints the mile back to Dan & Janet's house, just because he can. Now Alex is front flipping off waterfalls in the rain forest. How do I know this? I read it on another kid's Facebook. (Apparently 21st century missionaries use cyberspace.)

Oh YahYah, I see that you are not my baby anymore. You are not even a young man. You are a man. An international traveler. Seeking to hear from the Lord of the Universe. Looking for a plan for your life. Jump, Alex. Run and swim and seek and find. I am so proud of the leader that you have always been and I can't wait to see the leader who will come back to the States on the 4th of July. It's appropriate that you will return on Independence Day. I suspect it's the day you'll be free of your childhood. I might even have to drop the nickname.

You Call That a Compliment?

Don't even go to a reunion if you are looking for a compliment. I've made this mistake several times and it has never turned out the way I imagined. For instance, my husband is eleven years older than I am. When we went to his twentieth high school reunion, I expected to be fawned over as the adorable child bride. I can't count how many people asked, "Were you in my Math class? English? History?" The nerve of them to imply I was their age. I mean, c'mon, the lighting in here isn't that bad!

These days, people seem to be perfecting the art of pseudo-compliments. It's both compliment and insult in one. I hear a pseudo compliment fairly often and it really fries my bacon. People say, "You look great…for having five kids." Can't they just stop at "You look great?" Oh no, they can't. They don't. I guarantee that no one uses that line with Angelina Jolie.

One time this line really took the cake. One old friend said the "good for having five kids" line. This was promptly topped by the next guy. He said, "You think she looks good now? You should have seen her when she had only four kids!" Is that actually a compliment? C'mon, people! Men can be really slow. But women, oh, we have our own way of getting our point across.

Once a close friend said, "I know you think red is your color but it's not."

My mother said, "He's been waiting his whole life for you?"

A business associate patted my belly, which is like a permanent fanny pack in the front, and said, "It's not fat, it's your motherhood trophy."

And I know I'm not the only non-pregnant woman who has been hit with, "When is your baby due?" In my case, I gave her the evil eye and growled, "Six weeks ago." C'mon, lady, I was holding a newborn!

This is not meant to be a criticism. I know that wacky things slip out of my mouth on a daily basis. I always warn groups when I begin speaking that "I think I'm funny." That's the problem. To one person a humorous quip is a raging insult to another. I'm all for a great joke but not at someone else's expense. We've got to tone it down. The kids are listening. And they're taking notes.

What we do in moderation, the kids do in excess. We might know where to draw the line but they have yet to learn that skill. We need to model with words of encouragement and good cheer. Sure, laugh. Just don't laugh at people. It's a good life skill.

And while we're at it, let's resolve to zip it as far as the pseudo-compliments go. Remember that old adage: "If you don't have anything nice to say, don't say anything at all."

Let's give it a shot.

Jesus Took My Acrylic Nails

….and boy, did it hurt. Don't believe me? I'm serious. He took 'em, and I still miss 'em, and here's why.

Once I was going on a silly trip to Beverly Hills, of all places, and I was inordinately concerned with every single aspect of my physical body. Hair…highlighted. Wardrobe painstakingly assembled. Body….well, what's a mother of five to do? To the best of my ability, I was prepared.

Only one thing remained that truly revealed my full-time job as scrubwoman. My nails. In particular, one nail. 9 out of 10 were of decent length and once I got the grime out from under them, they appeared like a ladies' hand. One nail, however, was jagged and broken and just ruined my whole look."

My friend Clara innocently suggested that I get an acrylic nail. She explained that they could make the one broken nail match the other nine. Sign me up! I was there, my first big trip to the Nail Salon. Well, those nice folks were persuasive. And before you could say "Vanity", I had ten brand new acrylic nails on my natural nails. Not one, but ten. They all matched perfectly. A perfect set of fake nails. Do you see where this is headed? Do you think I experienced regret?

No way! I loved those Acrylic Nails. I loved them! I admired them. Stroked them. Looked at them a lot and I mean once every thirty seconds. Polished them. Flaunted them. Accepted compliments on their behalf.

I LOVED THEM!

As you might suspect, it got to be an obsession. It was crazy. I loved my nails. I spent time and money on them….time and money that I did not have to spend. And right away, like right when I got back from the trip, I felt the Holy Spirit whisper in my ear, "You're back home now, are you sure you need those acrylic nails?"

Heck yes, I was sure. So I started to bargain. I started making deals.

"I'll only get fills every two weeks."

"I deserve to pamper myself a little."

And here's the best one (hah, or the worst!):

"I'll pray the entire time I'm sitting there."

Because, after all, I loved the nails. And they looked great on me. They completed me…or so I imagined. And I was not alone. Others thought so, too. Once a lady from my church called. I barely knew her! She said that she always admired my natural-looking nails and wanted to know the name of my salon.

Hmmm…..natural looking…that was a bit of a wake-up call. I liked them because they were so perfect and fake-looking. Was natural-looking the goal, I wondered? This caused me to ponder while I got another fill.

When my dear friend Mark was dying, I bargained with God like never before. We prayed non-stop for him to live and as desperate people will, we started to try to sweeten the deal with "If you will only do this" prayers. We resolved to show God how serious we were by giving up things we loved in our lives.

His wife, Debi, gave up her beloved Diet Pepsi. I gave up…you guessed it….my acrylic nails. Mark was totally healed as only God can do. He received a perfect, strong, cancer-free body in heaven. After the funeral I went and got a new set of acrylic nails. Ooh, I had it bad.

Do you have acrylic nails? Or something else that you worship in your life? Yes, I can admit it, I worshiped those crazy, fake, plastic nails. When they were gone from my hands, I mourned. When they returned, I rejoiced.

Jesus took my acrylic nails. I started to realize that just possibly, I thought about those nails more than I thought about Him. (Ok, a lot more, I admit). Then I started to realize that I referred others to my Nail Salon more than I referred them to my. (Ok, a lot more.) I saw that my self-esteem was dependent on a French Manicure rather than the Word of God. That hurt.

One day, it just wasn't fun anymore. And I'll admit it, I was mad at the Lord for ruining my good time with my sexy nails. I prayed that the Lord would take away my desire and admiration for my acrylic nails. He didn't. I still wanted them. I'd get them back today if He'd let me. What the Lord did, though, was tell me, "I'm all you need." He told me, "It will be okay." So I took the nails off. And they stayed off.

Then when I looked at my sore, weak, tiny baby nails that were under the acrylics, I thought of Christ. I remembered why I took them off. It took nearly a year for my strong, natural nails to come back. That gave me ample time to think.

He loves me enough to say, "That's enough." Just like a Dad says to a whining child who has had too many treats, "That's enough!" I was scolded.

And I am so grateful. Now all I want is a tummy tuck.

The Mother I Imagined I'd Be

My friend Amy and I still talk about the mother we imagined we'd be. She was really super great. She never lost her patience or for that matter, her car keys. She never yelled at the kids "Hurry up!" She didn't have to yell to hurry because she was never in a hurry. She had everything planned in advance. She had outfits laid out on the beds, library books all together on a shelf and car keys on the hook. She was awesome.

She disappeared when the kids came. She was replaced with someone who had brain cells leaking out with the breast milk. She lost her job to the one who woke up crabby, locked the keys in the car and forgot the diaper bag on the day the baby's messy diaper exploded up his back. She lost her job to me.

Now I think the mother I imagined I would be was actually a grandmother. She was patient because she was not lactating or homeschooling or having to wear her husband's jeans to Wal-Mart because they were the only clean pants in the house that would fit over her belly. She sang songs because she was not worried about transferring money between accounts before another check bounced. She made cookies because she wanted to make a memory and she wouldn't be bothered by granulated sugar crunching underfoot in the kitchen. She wouldn't be bothered because her cleaning lady would sweep it right up.

I said goodbye to Imaginary Mother when I realized that she was as much of a fantasy as the mom on a Hallmark commercial. I started planning on being the World's Best Grandmother. I have all the beloved Thomas the Tank Engine toys tucked away for when they start to arrive. (Please, God, give us some time; I'm not that ready yet!) I haven't given up my dreams completely, however. I do want my kids to leave home with something they'll treasure forever. (No, not a scrapbook, though I'll fill their car trunk with those!) The gift I want them to leave with is an abiding faith.

There is a teenager in the Bible who has a strong faith. He traced it back through his mom and grandmom. I am inspired. I may not have passed on great table manners or the necessity of a well-worded and timely thank you note. But by golly, I think I've shown a real, living faith. If only the kids could catch what I have.

Once I told a friend that I wish I could download my faith straight to my kids. "Think of it, it would go straight into their hearts and minds, everything I believe."

He paused and responded, "But the download would also include every experience you had and every lesson you learned on the way to your faith. Are you positive you want to download all that?"

Downloaded faith cancelled. All I can do is live the faith. I can't pass it on. I can only live it out. Timothy was challenged to fan into flames the gift of God. That's where we can help. Each child is born with a spark. It's a tiny burning ember of faith and hope and trust and love. It's child-like faith. It doesn't require a degree or an explanation. It just is.

We can fan the flame into a roaring fire of faith. Beware! The ember can be easily extinguished. There have been many times that I am in danger of extinguishing their spark. My sharp tongue is as effective as a bucket of water on their teeny flame. You just know that Lois and Eunice (Timothy's grandmother and mother) weren't saying things like, "If you weren't so lazy, you would have finished that by now." I'm in Work in Progress, too.

Fan into flames the gift of God in the little people. Fan, fan, fan! That's what Imaginary Mother would do. She would use her words to build up, not tear down. She would remember that it's better to listen than to speak. She would pray because heck, there's nothing better she can do. In this way, I can be Imaginary Mother. I can do those things. And so can you.

Fan the flame!

I Quit

I got a new job once. I went for one day. No one talked to me at lunch. The boss criticized me for chewing gum at the office. I could tell he was going to be a real treat to work for. He handed me a stack of manuals to read and memorize. It was the longest eight hours of my life. At the end of the day, after discussing it with my husband, I quit. It was pretty satisfying. The job annoyed me so I quit.

Parenting isn't like that. It's a job that has the capacity to annoy me every day. Often no one talks to me. Or if they do, it's to present a list of demands. "Pick me up now!" the voice on the other end of the phone growled when I picked it up. "Excuse me!" I retorted to my son, "Do I work for you?" The truth is, I do.

When the kids were little I would be completely out of any final drip of kindness, concern or interest after 8 p.m. I would say, "Mom is off duty." That was my fantasy response. If I had eight to twelve hours to recharge, I'd be an awesome mother come morning. Alas, I'm sad to report. Mom is never off duty!

I kept trying to go Off the Clock, though. I reasoned that once I had said good-night that was it. And some night, I didn't even want to say good-night. I wanted to run screaming into the night. I wanted to go back and get a job where the biggest issue was if I was allowed to chew gum or not.

It's an exhausting job. Our pay is in Butterfly Kisses, but that doesn't cover the cell phone bill. Choosing to stay home with our kids has meant a wealth of attention, supervision, love and guidance poured into their lives. It's also meant walking a tightrope of finances and strain as we squeeze the most out of every penny. I always say about mothering, "The pay is lousy but the benefits are great." And I almost always mean it.

The benefits are in the future, however. Parenting is sort of like a 401K. It's going to pay off in the future. We hope. For today, we need to keep making our deposits into the account. We need to trust there will be a payoff one day. The endless depositing can wear you down.

Don't give up! When I squeeze parenting advice from the Bible, I blow past the verses that address spanking. I want to get encouragement for my own marathon race of parenting. I need something for me. I found something in there that has encouraged me. It's a verse that says, *"Don't get weary of doing good because at the proper time we'll reap a harvest if we don't give up."*

I love this. I love it because it states very clearly our temptation to just get sick and tired of doing good. We might just be plain exhausted of the repetition of it all. Parenting is so daily.

Did you brush your teeth?

Did you hand in your homework?

Did you send Grandma an email?

Did you feed the dogs?

Did you apologize to your brother?

Day in, day out. It's exhausting. And that's just the day-to-day stuff. Many days a crisis will be added on your To Do list. Maybe it's a child up all night coughing. Or one who comes home with a note from the teacher…again. Maybe it's a teenager's disrespect or a toddler's broken arm. Or, God forbid, something worse. A diagnosis. An addiction. A death.

It will wear you down. You will feel worn down. You will feel like giving in. But don't do it. Don't give up! There's a promise ahead. There's a guarantee. Hold on. There is a harvest ahead....if we don't give up.

What might that harvest look like? I love to dream. I dream of my pure daughters on their wedding days; they give their hearts to their one and only true loves.

I dream of my sons as they graduate. They have pursued a course of study with a passion and they will go into the world equipped to make a difference.

I dream of them having their own children and finally realizing that their Mom and Dad did the very best they could. I dream they will appreciate us one day.

It will be a day of harvest when they do. So take heart. It's always too soon to quit. Parenting is forever. And the benefits are eternal.

Confessions of a Former Know-It-All

I'm scared of people who know it all. I know a few of them. I recognize the species. Because, well, I used to be one. I knew it all. At least, I thought I did. When I was younger, hoooo baby, you could not tell me anything. I knew it all. I look back now and blush. If I had addresses, I'd send out lots of sympathy cards. I'd write to everyone who used to work with me, for one. I'd say...

Sorry you had to work with me in the 80's.
I know I was really obnoxious.
Thanks for not throwing me out the window of our
high story office building.
Blessings! Martie

I bet some people are still mad. Like one lady chased me into the bathroom once and yelled at me through the stall. She told me I was young and I didn't know what I was saying. I sat on the toilet and thought about how wrong she was. Sorry, Kate. To Kate, I should send flowers.

My gosh, the moral fiber I imagined that I had! The stand that I took on so many issues! Ok, it's a tiny bit cute now, to remember how very brilliant I felt when I argued with adults. I felt powerful! I felt right! I could not be dissuaded! On the other hand, now that I have teenagers and have those arguments in reverse, it's not all that cute. It's annoying.

When did I figure out that I didn't know it all? I guess it started when I met the Lord. You see, the very first thing I learned about God was this. *"He removes our past transgressions as far as the East is from the West."*

This was both reassuring and humiliating. It was reassuring because I was dragging a lot of baggage around with me. I wasn't quite sure how I'd ever be free of it. It was great to know that it could be sent through some heavenly FedEx to the other end of the earth. It was humiliating because if God was going to perform that service for me, gosh, it meant He knew what all the transgressions were. He knew it all. It wasn't me who knew it all, it was God. Gosh, that was painful....but freeing at the same time.

Well, the more I grow in the Lord, the more I realize that I don't know it all. I hardly know anything. But I'm psyched because God really does know everything. And He still loves us. He knows what happened in the past. He knows what will happen in the future. He even knows every word we're going to say, before we say it.

When I found that Scripture, I was fascinated! Every word? Before we say it? To test this out, I shouted out a swear word, a really bad one, really fast. And I felt the Lord kind of smirking, with a knowing grin on His face. *"I knew you were going to say that,"* He said.

You can't get away from the Lord. And that's a great thing. So now I know that I don't know much. And I'm pretty relaxed about it. See, the view is nicer from the "Don't Know It All" side of the fence. You don't have to always be arguing. You don't have to think how stupid everyone else is all the time. You can just hang out, and love people.

So now when I meet a Know-It-All, I just smile. And throw up a silent prayer that the Lord will grab hold of them, and save them from themselves, like He did with me. I'm really grateful. I don't know much...but I do know Him.

Turns out, that's All.

How to Make My Lord Your Lord

I grew up going to church. We went almost every Sunday. This was a real drag for me because there were no cute boys in our church. Sadly, that is what I remember most. Confirmation class was practically torture because of the no cute boy factor. I tried to talk myself into having a crush on the one 8th grade boy in that class, but to no avail. I grew up in church, but I wasn't really there, if you know what I mean.

College was a four-year party. Career was when I started to pay attention to life around me. I was sad, confused and tired. "If this is all there is to life, I'm not sure I want to stick around." I remember often having that thought. I would drive down the beautiful towns on the Main Line outside of Philadelphia, and look at all the lovely stone churches. I thought there might be something for me within their walls, but I was too intimidated to go see for myself.

So I started researching other world philosophies which might add significance to my lonely life. New Age was interesting with its emphasis on self. But the crystals just seemed ridiculous to me and I knew that it wasn't the truth. Co-workers and dear friends were Jewish. That fascinated me. I loved the holy days and knew as much about them as some of my friends. The process to convert was arduous, though, and I knew from the outset that I wasn't really committed…I just wanted to be part of the club.

At the end of 1989, something wacky happened. I met a cute man on a plane. We talked for the entire five hour flight. Although he lived in a different state, he offered to drive up and take me out to lunch sometime. I was skeptical but the conversation had been great. I said yes and we exchanged phone numbers on the back of our boarding passes. His name was Dave.

Dave did indeed call and drive from Annapolis to Philadelphia to take me to lunch. The lunch turned to dinner and the conversation deepened. Over dinner he started to talk about his faith in Jesus Christ. I felt very uncomfortable. In our church growing up, we talked about God but not about Christ. We certainly didn't speak of Christ as if He was someone we knew, who was in the same restaurant, and even in the same conversation. I felt sad because I thought this guy Dave was pretty cool but now he turned out to be some type of Jesus Freak. But something in me agreed to another date. It was only a number of weeks before we both felt that we were falling in love. Dave then gave me an unusual gift; at least I thought it was odd. He gave me my first Bible.

"Start at the Gospels…Matthew, Mark, Luke and John," he advised.

"You can't start a book in the middle!" I scolded.

"It's actually the beginning of the second section," Dave assured me. "It's allowed."

It was a crazy ride. Some of the stories seemed a bit familiar to me, from my days in Sunday school, but most of it seemed very new. I remember thinking, "This Jesus is cool!" He was not at all what I had expected. He was full of love and compassion and peace. He didn't rush and He didn't judge. He listened and He calmed the storm. I started to fall in love…this time with this Jesus that Dave knew and loved. Yet something was holding me back. Those college years and all the choices that I had made, well, it didn't seem like such a party anymore. I had deep regrets. I imagined that those old choices would keep me from a new way. My deepest desire was that I could push a "re-do" button and start a whole new life. I wished that I could be new but I remembered with shame and disgust some of my earlier actions. If I felt that way, what would a holy God think of what I had done? I felt stuck.

Dave and his whole family prayed. It wasn't that they wanted me to join their club. It was that they wanted me to have the freedom they experienced. Dave invited me to a Christian seminar and while some of it was poignant, much of it was boring. Attending after a long day at work, I often dozed off. Then, one night, I heard some things that cut through my fatigue and my anxiety.

- *"Your past transgressions are as far as the East is from the West."*
- *"You can be born again."*
- *"In Christ you are a new creation…the old is gone, the new has come."*
- *"Christ died once for all."*
- *"You are forgiven."*

These promises from the Bible were exactly what I had hoped and dreamed of. I could be new. I would be accepted. I could press the re-do button and enter into a new life with Christ. His sacrifice was enough…I just needed to believe and receive. I wasn't alone! "All have sinned and fall short of the glory of God." His death cancelled out my sin forever. I raised my hand, like a little kid at school, and received. It was that easy. It was that complicated.

Since then, I've grown in the knowledge of Christ and love Him, the lover of my soul. I find Him everywhere I go…in nature, in His Word, in the kids. I want to share the joy and freedom that I found with everyone I meet. It's my very favorite thing to talk about. I'd love to share with you. Oh yes, and I'm sure you figured it out….Dave and I got married ten months after we met, courtesy of U.S. Air and the eternal God who has a great sense of humor.

It's Not About Me

The best speech I ever gave was titled "It's Not About Me." It was a joke. You see, every single example, every story, every line was about me. I only claimed it was not about me. That was the joke. My false modesty. However, the lesson was valid. I had finally figured out, in my thirties, that the world did not revolve around me. It was good to know.

There are two types of vanity. One is thinking very highly of yourself. The other is thinking you are nothing. Both of these are forms of pride. Whether you suffer from one or the other, you need to repeat these words, "It's not about me!" You are here by order of the King on an important assignment to Planet Earth. You have been gifted and skilled. You are called to help and bless others. That's what it's about.

The Bible says that we should not think of ourselves more highly than we ought, but with sober (realistic) judgment. The converse, of course, is that we should not think of ourselves as less than we really are. Low self esteem is pride that goes underground. It still shows that you think it's all about you…just in a negative, not positive light. We can only repair our self-esteem by taking "self" out of the mix. Instead, we need to have God-esteem. This is what I've learned….

It's about Him, not me. He made me. He called me out of darkness. He calls me his beloved. My own emotions may lie to me. I know they do. I have never been invited to speak somewhere without getting absolute flop sweats the day of the presentation. I feel in my heart, "They don't really want me here. This is a big mistake." Those sentiments feel very, very real. (I've had to pray in earnest to make myself get out of my car and walk into a meeting that I've been invited to! Doesn't that sound ridiculous?) It <u>feels</u> real, but it's <u>not real</u>.

Yet, I can't persuade myself by using my own wisdom and counsel. It just doesn't work that way. I have to take it to a higher authority. I know how I feel...but what is the truth? There is Truth with a capital T. It is not what the world says. It is not what Glamour magazine says. It is not what your high school coach says. It is not what your boss, your mother or your husband says about you.

The absolute Truth is found in God's word. The Truth is that God calls me His workmanship, His poem. He promises to love me with an everlasting love. He assures me that He will never leave me or forsake me. He is enthralled by my beauty! He is my Lord! That is the truth. That is God-esteem.

The secret, then, is to not evaluate yourself by the mirror or by comparing yourself with others. (What they are wearing? Saying? Thinking? Doing?)

You do have an audience...but it's not the one you think you have. You have an Audience of One. Jesus Christ is the One. He is the Way. He is the Truth. He is the Life. He is the Word, the living Word. Who does the Word say I am? That's the only thing that matters.

Who Am I in Christ?

I Am:

A Child of God. *1 John 3:10*
Above and not beneath. *Deuteronomy 28:13*
The apple of my Father's eye. *Psalm 17:8*
The aroma of Christ. *2 Corinthians 2:15*
Called by God. *Hebrews 5:4*
Chosen by God. *1 Thessalonians 1:4*
Christ's ambassador. *2 Corinthians 5:20*
Comforted by God. *2 Corinthians 1:4*
Complete in Christ. *1 John 2:5*
Crucified with Christ. *Galatians 2:20*
Forgiven of all my sin. *Matthew 26:28*
God's field and God's building. *1 Corinthians 3:9*
His faithful follower. *Revelation 17:14*
Light of the world. *Matthew 5:14*
Loved by God. *Romans 1:7*
Salt of the Earth. *Matthew 5:13*
Set free. *John 8:6*
Strong in Christ. *1 Peter 5:10*
Temple of the Holy Spirit. *1 Corinthians 6:19*

These are the promises for believers in Jesus Christ. There are many, many more. Make the Truth your filter for how you act and how you feel. Surround yourself with the Word and do not rely on your emotions or what others say. Build your house…and your business…on the rock, Jesus Christ.

Copyright Jennifer Fountain 2009

This list comes from my friend Jenn Fountain. She has designed these affirmations into beautiful magnets that you can put on your fridge. They are a great way to remind yourself every day of the truth of who you are in Christ. They are an awesome way to teach your children the Truth, too.

To order sets of these affirmations, log on to www.jennfountain.com.

About the author

Martie Smith Byrd is an encourager. She loves to speak to groups large and small. She shares with humor and spice on a variety of topics including parenting, faith, business and life. She was an award-winning advertising copywriter in Philadelphia until she began her family. She had five children in six years while maintaining a highly successful home-based business. Martie retired as a Director with a vibrant team to focus on writing and speaking. She is a follower of Christ and loves to let His light shine wherever she goes!

Martie grew up in Simsbury, Connecticut. She and her beloved husband, Dave, met on a plane in Texas. They have five gorgeous and talented children: Alex, Daniel, Trevor, Caroline and Julia. They live in beautiful Roanoke, Virginia, the Star City of the South.

Martie is a monthly columnist in the Southwest Virginia regional magazine, Bella. Her column, "Welcome to my World," is about her household of teens. She is the author of two books: *Little Ideas, Big Results* and *The Kids Drank Pickle Juice*. For copies, please contact the author directly. There is a wonderful quantity discount!

Martie would love to come speak to your group or organization. To contact her with a speaking request, please email martiebyrd@yahoo.com. To read more encouragement, log on to www.martiebyrd.com.

My Inspiration

Trevor, Julia, Alex, Caroline and Daniel

Photo by Dave "Happy Daddy" Byrd
Mother's Day 2009

Shine Like Stars

A ministry of encouragement for women

Shine like stars
In the universe
As you hold out
The word of life.

Philippians 2:15-16

www.martiebyrd.com
(540) 563-9898
martiebyrd@yahoo.com

CANDID REVIEWS

Martie has a lively and humorous style that is very engaging. She is practical in her approach to a topic - she shares principles and practices in a way that can be easily grasped and applied by her listeners. She speaks from personal experience, giving her credibility with her audience.

Martie is REAL.

Barbara McCandless

"Martie's words and passion for the Lord blessed the women of our church in so many ways. Though we were only with her for a weekend, the impact has been far reaching! We could feel and see her relationship with Jesus Christ in every word, every prayer and every funny moment of the weekend. Martie, thank you for sharing your experiences and your heart with us! It was an incredibly moving and inspirational weekend, a retreat that changed lives and hearts!"

Kris Kuester

"Your leadership, talent and enthusiasm transformed our women's retreat into a weekend of godly renewal! You have certainly found your calling. May God continue to bless you and your family to permit you to serve Him in such amazing ways!"

Cheryl Lafferty

www.ingramcontent.com/pod-product-compliance
Lightning Source LLC
Chambersburg PA
CBHW032001080426
42735CB00007B/471